Understanding Anore~
in Males

Because anorexia nervosa has historically been viewed as a disorder that impacts women and girls, there has been little focus on the conceptualization and treatment of males suffering from this complex disorder. *Understanding Anorexia Nervosa in Males* provides a structure for understanding the male side of the equation combined with practical resources to guide clinical intervention. Presented using an integrative framework that draws on recent research and organizes information from multiple domains into a unified understanding of the interconnected issues at hand, this informative new text provides a comprehensive approach to understanding and treating a widely unrecognized population.

Tom Wooldridge, PsyD is an assistant professor at Golden Gate University, where he chairs the Psychology Department. He is also an Executive Director at the National Association for Males with Eating Disorders (NAMED), a member of the editorial board of *Eating Disorders: The Journal of Treatment and Prevention*, and publishes widely on eating disorders, particularly as they manifest in males, as well as other topics including pro-anorexia forums and the uses of technology in psychoanalytic treatment. He is a candidate at the Psychoanalytic Institute of Northern California and in private practice in Berkeley, California.

Praise for *Understanding Anorexia Nervosa in Males*

Understanding Anorexia Nervosa in Males provides a fresh, broad, and clinically sophisticated approach to anorexia nervosa in general, and to males with anorexia nervosa in particular. This outstanding new book engages the reader from the first page to the last. Several novel concepts that add perspective to the field are presented for the first time. After a review of all the current approaches to the treatment of anorexia nervosa (and the references are superb), the author critically examines these approaches and proposes an approach to engagement and alliance with patients. He clarifies with patient examples the ambivalence of patients suffering from anorexia nervosa, allowing the reader to step in the shoes of the patient cognitively, culturally, and physically. His discussion of negative vs. positive constraints is nowhere else treated with this clarity and clinical utility. The chapter on Cyberspace with its comparison of the risks vs. benefits of pro-ana sites for males is provocative and speaks with compassion to the alienation of males with anorexia nervosa. No other source addresses so well the spiritual framework and milieu of anorexia in males. Don't expect a simplistic "how-to" guide, but do expect a comprehensive, fresh, and challenging new view of anorexia nervosa in males that brings an integrative approach to the understanding and treatment of anorexia nervosa in males. A potential classic that takes away your breath with its freshness and applicability, touching on topics not found elsewhere. Strongly recommended for all clinicians and families.

—Arnold Andersen, MD, professor emeritus of psychiatry, University of Iowa, former director and founder of Eating and Weight Disorders Program, University of Iowa, Johns Hopkins Hospital, author, *Making Weight: Men's Conflicts with Food, Weight, Shape, & Appearance* and *Eating Disorders: A Guide to Medical Care and Complications*

This groundbreaking book illuminates the less explored, but nonetheless problematic issue of male anorexia. Wooldridge identifies existing treatments to anorexia and finds them wanting with respect to the treatment of males and calls for a new, integrative approach that specifically speaks to boys and men. Infused with tasty morsels of research and theory, he compellingly posits an approach using a multi-faceted framework with accessible clinical vignettes that help us think in adaptive ways – not only to the complexity of this disorder, but to how we can help our patients recognize their hunger and relational yearnings to eat and be fed, as they learn – with our help – that they can speak about the often unspeakable.

—Jean Petrucelli, PhD, director and co-founder of the Eating Disorders, Compulsions and Addictions Service, William Alanson White Institute, editor of *Body-States: Interpersonal & Relational Perspectives on the Treatment of Eating Disorders* and co-editor of *Hungers and Compulsions: The Psychodynamic Treatment of Eating Disorders and Addictions*

Tom Wooldridge's *Understanding Anorexia in Males* is a thoroughly researched, sensitively focused, and lively systematic review of all treatment modalities essential for guiding therapy in the 21st century. Readers will particularly resonate with and learn from the clinical examples and actual dialogues between patient and therapist that Dr. Wooldridge boldly includes in each chapter. This gem is an essential reference for all who aim to understand and to assist men in their recovery from a severe eating disorder. Highly recommended to students, family members, and patients who want to learn more about the subject, too.

—Kathryn J. Zerbe, MD, FAED, author, *The Body Betrayed: Women, Eating Disorders and Treatment* and *Integrated Treatment of Eating Disorders: Beyond the Body Betrayed*, clinical professor, Oregon Health and Science University, training and supervising analyst, Oregon Psychoanalytic Institute

Understanding Anorexia Nervosa in Males: An Integrative Approach fills an empty hole in the eating disorder literature, shedding light on a subject that we have ignored for far too long. With a historical and cultural perspective Tom Wooldridge contextualizes male anorexia, challenging the myth that men are immune to eating disorders, and describes how their unique experiences of ambivalence, shame, and stigma keep them in the closet. The multidimensional integrative treatment approach provides a framework to identify and address systemic, biological, cultural, spiritual, and psychodynamic factors and their interactions in the illness process as well as in treatment. Case material enlivens this well-written and clinically useful resource for anyone who wants to understand male anorexia – and that should be every practicing clinician, specialist or generalist. It's about time to make men with eating disorders more visible to both the public and professional communities so they can be identified and treated. Wooldridge does just that in this excellent and timely book.

—Margo Maine, PhD, FAED, CEDS, a founder and adviser of the National Eating Disorders Association and founding fellow of the Academy for Eating Disorders, Maine, author of *Treatment of Eating Disorders: Bridging the Research–Practice Gap*; *Effective Clinical Practice in the Treatment of Eating Disorders*; *The Body Myth*; *Father Hunger*; and *Body Wars*, recipient of the 2015 NEDA Lifetime Achievement Award, member of the Renfrew Clinical Advisory Board and the Renfrew Foundation Conference Committee

Tom Wooldridge has written a masterful review of males with eating disorders that will be a resource for those working with this population for many years to come. Wooldridge's book provides an "integrative model" for understanding this under-identified and appreciated illness in boys and men. His expertise comes through without question, addressing treatment issues compassionately and comprehensively. A must-read for clinicians working in the field.

—Theodore Weltzin, MD, FAED, CEDS, regional medical director, eating disorders, Rogers Memorial Hospital

For many years, anorexia nervosa has been conceptualized as a "female" illness, a misnomer which has stymied illness recognition and treatment, in addition to stigmatized males with this illness. With research slowly recognizing the increasing prevalence of anorexia nervosa in males, several key questions arise. Do males with anorexia nervosa differ from females with this illness? How do we recognize anorexia nervosa in males? How do we treat this syndrome in males? Dr. Wooldridge's illuminative compendium *Understanding Anorexia Nervosa in Males* provides a comprehensive guide to working with anorexia nervosa in males. Dr. Wooldridge's renowned expertise in this area offers a unique window into understanding the cultural, biological, systemic, and spiritual underpinnings of this syndrome in males. Further, the core focus on clinical applications throughout bring the complex theories to life, and make them immediately relatable to readers. I will definitely be recommending this book to colleagues and patients, and I think this will serve as a milestone publication in our field.

—Stuart B. Murray, PhD, assistant professor, University of California, San Francisco, co-executive director, National Association for Males with Eating Disorders

Understanding Anorexia Nervosa in Males: An Integrative Approach is a first of its kind, and a much needed treatment manual that integrates various psychotherapeutic approaches to address this growing life-threatening disorder. To date, there exist only a few professional articles that focus on the treatment of males with anorexia and a few books aimed at muscle dysmorphism. This new volume is a comprehensive, up-to-date work, which is a major contribution to understanding the diagnosis and treatment of anorexia among men.

—Ray Lemberg, PhD, editor of *Eating Disorders: A Reference Sourcebook*, co-editor of *Current Findings on Males with Eating Disorders*, associate editor, *Eating Disorders: The Journal of Treatment & Prevention*

Understanding Anorexia Nervosa in Males

An Integrative Approach

Tom Wooldridge, PsyD

Routledge
Taylor & Francis Group

NEW YORK AND LONDON

First published 2016
by Routledge
711 Third Avenue, New York, NY 10017

and by Routledge
2 Park Square, Milton Park, Abingdon, Oxon, OX14 4RN

Routledge is an imprint of the Taylor & Francis Group, an informa business

© 2016 Taylor & Francis

Library of Congress Cataloging in Publication Data
A catalog record for this book has been requested

ISBN: 978-1-138-94930-0 (hbk)
ISBN: 978-1-138-94932-4 (pbk)
ISBN: 978-1-315-66913-7 (ebk)

Typeset in Sabon
by HWA Text and Data Management, London

Printed and bound in the United States of America by Publishers Graphics,
LLC on sustainably sourced paper.

For Caroline

Contents

Figures

Foreword

Leigh Cohn

Very few people get anorexia nervosa, and most who do are female. So, why is this book important? Because millions of males develop eating disorders (Wade, Keski-Rahkonen, & Hudson, 2011) and there are no current treatment manuals devoted to them. Ever since eating disorders first manifested as a field in the 1970s and 80s, males have been marginalized.

A brief look at the past 50 or so years shows the evolution of this dynamic. In the Introduction of this book, Tom Wooldridge mentions the earliest clinical descriptions of anorexia nervosa, which include cases of boys and young men, with examples from the 1600s to the 1860s. Then he writes, "Over the next 100 years, however, males are almost unmentioned in the literature." So, let's pick up the story from there.

In the 1960s, individuals with anorexia nervosa were treated in medical or psychiatric settings, and only severe cases were diagnosed. Both genders were treated, though then, as now, the majority of cases were female. A cultural revolution was beginning in the United States and other Western societies, which included both the Feminist Movement and the Twiggy Era, when the Marilyn Monroe-esque, full-figured shape gave way to thinness as the standard of idealized beauty. The diet industry flourished, and it almost exclusively targeted women. At that time, men were still encouraged to be fit and muscular, as they had been since the iconic Charles Atlas booklets became the rage in the 40s, but a new, lean hippie look was starting to emerge.

The psychological issues of anorexia nervosa were only beginning to be explored by psychiatrists such as Gerald Russell and Arthur Crisp in the United Kingdom and Hilde Bruch and Karl Menninger (who is less known for his work in this area) in the United States. Treatment modalities usually focused on weight restoration, family issues, trauma, and depression. However, more and more young women were showing up in hospitals, and their obsession with thinness began to tilt assessments away from merely looking at percentage of weight lost and amenorrhea.

Another curious symptom was also noticed in the mid-70s: individuals were using self-induced vomiting for weight loss. While this was a widely known technique for jockeys and wrestlers – I personally remember wrestling teammates throwing up in the showers in the late 60s – it was being employed by young women. Although this behavior was thought to be "an ominous variant of anorexia nervosa" (Russell, 1979), before the end of the decade "bulimarexia" was described in *Psychology Today* by Boskind-Lodahl and Sirlin (1977) and by Russell, who introduced bulimia nervosa in the academic literature (1979). These publications only examined women.

No one seemed too bothered that guys were "puking to make weight," but when young women were telling stories of binge eating enormous amounts of food and then sticking their fingers down their throats – several times every day – the world started to take notice. In the intervening years, the numbers of women presenting with bulimia spiked, but the reasons for this sharp increase in prevalence are not certain. Most eating disorders specialists would agree that sociocultural pressure to be thin, combined with feminist messages of personal empowerment, had a lot to do with it.

I remember how the shift in cultural awareness occurred, because my wife, Lindsey Hall, and I published a booklet about her recovery from the binge–purge syndrome (1980) and began giving workshops on college campuses and eventually writing books on the topic. A year later, she became the first person to appear on national television discussing bulimia, as information about eating disorders began appearing in the media. Soon after that, we founded the *Eating Disorders Bookshelf Catalogue*, and for the next 35 years, we reviewed virtually 99 percent of the books published in the field. Additionally, I saw the phenomenal interest in the books we were marketing, and direct mail campaigns to college counselors and health centers had staggering results compared to industry standards.

Essentially, every book that came out through the 80s viewed eating disorders primarily as women's problems. *Fat is a Feminist Issue* by Susie Orbach, *The Obsession* by Kim Chernin, and *Making Peace with Food* by Susan Kano were among the most popular titles. Likewise, eating disorders in the general vernacular took on a feminist perspective, as did many treatment approaches. As an editor and publisher, I encouraged authors to use feminine pronouns, and I admit that I was just as convinced as everyone else that men needed to take a back seat.

When *Males with Eating Disorders* by Arnold Andersen came out in 1990, it was met with little fanfare or attention. Andersen routinely contributed chapters to professional text anthologies, but his was the *only* book devoted to this population until the 21st century. In the mid-90s, I noticed an alarming increase in phone calls to our book company from men with eating disorders, parents of sons who were struggling, and wives concerned about their husbands. I spoke to a television producer who had been bingeing and purging since high school, a physician who exercised addictively and was concerned about his low weight, an office worker who topped the scales at over 400 pounds as the result of uncontrollable binge eating, and a friend who became obsessed with eliminating dietary fat from everything he ate. I heard from Lindsey that the son of a couple we knew was seeing a therapist for anorexia nervosa, which was embarrassingly denied by his father when I asked how the son's recovery was progressing. Eventually, I concluded that a self-help book for males was sorely needed, and I approached Arnold Andersen and Tom Holbrook, who ran the only men's eating disorders program in the country, to collaborate.

When *Making Weight* (2000) hit bookshelves, coincidentally, *The Adonis Complex* (Pope, Phillips, & Olivardia, 2000) came out at the same time, and I was convinced that males with eating disorders would begin to see parity in recognition and treatment. Both books received significant attention in the national media, but sales were definitely not spectacular. Most therapists weren't seeing many male patients, and most articles and websites stated that 90 percent of cases involved females, a statistic taken from Andersen's studies in the 80s. We upgraded that figure in *Making Weight*, estimating the incidence of males with eating disorders to be in the 25–30 percent range, which was confirmed in 2007 (Hudson, Hiripi, Pope, & Kessler, 2007). Nonetheless, that old 90 percent female: 10 percent male ratio has stubbornly persisted on the Internet and even in many academic articles. For over 15 years, I spoke about males and eating disorders at professional conferences, colleges, prep schools, and hospitals, spreading the word; but my talks were generally met with ambivalence – except there were usually a couple of guys who approached me afterwards to share their own struggles.

When we released *Making Weight*, there were over 1,000 books related to eating disorders in print, yet less than 1 percent focused on males. Similarly, when I conducted a PubMed search for the term "eating disorders" in abstracts from journal articles written before 2000, there were 3,168 results, but the term "males" was included in only 5.4 percent of them. Even today, I can count the professional books published on males and eating disorders on one hand, and the ratio of journal articles on males has increased by a mere 2 percent over the past 15 years. Access to specialized treatment for males has also been sparse, and though most eating disorders therapists may have had a few male patients, there has been little professional training in this area. Unfortunately, a typical layperson's response when I mention my own work with males and eating disorders is of surprise, "Oh, I thought mainly teenage girls get that disease."

In 2014, Ray Lemberg and I coedited *Current Findings on Males with Eating Disorders*, which included "An Overview of Anorexia Nervosa in Males" by Tom Wooldridge and Pauline Lytle. Although the book provides a fairly comprehensive summary of research, it only has a couple of treatment chapters. So, really, this book by Wooldridge, *Understanding Anorexia Nervosa in Males: An Integrated Approach* is the first clinical manual for a grossly neglected population. I've had an opportunity to work closely with Tom on the executive board of the National Association for Males with Eating Disorders, and I have been impressed by his knowledge of the subject and superb writing skills.

Why is this book important? It is leading the way for therapists to grasp the unique concerns of males with anorexia nervosa and to help them recover from this insidious eating disorder. In the near future, I hope to see more books that address bulimia, binge eating disorder, male body image, and the myriad of clinical issues that boys and men face. Undoubtedly, we will also see books devoted to eating disorders in the lesbian, gay, bisexual, transgender and queer (LGBTQ) community, which has been nearly entirely ignored in the literature. I'm not advocating gender neutrality when it comes to understanding and treating eating disorders, because men and women have fundamental differences. That's why we must have treatment handbooks that address more populations than just women and girls. For now, this book is a good start.

Leigh Cohn, MAT, CEDS is the publisher of Gürze Books, Editor-in-Chief of *Eating Disorders: The Journal of Treatment and Prevention*, coauthor of several books, and President of the National Association for Males with Eating Disorders.

References

Andersen, A.E. (Ed.) (1990). *Males with eating disorders*. New York: Brunner/ Mazel.

Andersen, A., Cohn, L. & Holbrook, T. (2000). *Making weight: Healing men's conflicts with food, weight, shape & appearance*. Carlsbad, CA: Gürze Books.

Boskind-Lodahl, M. & Sirlin, J. (1977). The gorging-purging syndrome. *Psychology Today*, March. 50–52.

Chernin, K. (1981). *The obsession*. New York: Harper & Row.

Cohn, L. & Lemberg, R. (Eds.) (2014). *Current findings on males with eating disorders*. New York: Routledge.

Hall, L. & Cohn, L. (1980). *Eat without fear: A true story of the gorge-purge syndrome*. Carlsbad, CA: Gürze Books.

Hudson, J., Hiripi, E., Pope, H. & Kessler, R. (2007). The prevalence and correlates of eating disorders in the National Comorbidity Survey Replication. *Biological Psychiatry*, 61(3), 348–358.

Kano, S. (1989). *Making peace with food*. New York: HarperCollins.

Orbach, S. (1978). *Fat is a feminist issue*. New York: Putnam.

Pope, H., Phillips, K. & Olivardia, R. (2000). *The Adonis complex: How to identify, treat and prevent body obsession in men and boys*. New York: Simon & Schuster, Inc.

Russell, G. (1979). Bulimia nervosa: an ominous variant of anorexia nervosa. *Psychological Medicine*, August, 429–448.

Wade, T. D., Keski-Rahkonen, A. & Hudson, J. (2011). Epidemiology of eating disorders. In M. Tsuang and M. Tohen (Eds.), *Textbook in psychiatric epidemiology* (3rd ed.) (pp. 343–360). New York: Wiley.

Foreword

Roberto Olivardia

It is an all too familiar reaction. "Wow, you specialize in treating *boys and men* with eating disorders? I thought that was something only girls suffered from." I take the other person down the road of my journey in the field of males with eating disorders, beginning with my interest as a college student at Tufts University, where two men had confided in me that they secretly struggled with a disorder that had culturally only been reserved (unfortunately) for women. They felt an intense sense of shame, feeling as if their masculinity was diminished, while they were immersed in self-loathing around their bodies. It inspired me to write a senior thesis on eating disorders in college men. My thesis committee gave me the caveat that the ads I placed in college newspapers in the Boston area may not yield enough interest, perhaps due to low numbers of men who fulfilled the DSM-IV criteria of anorexia nervosa, bulimia nervosa or binge eating disorder. I should have a Plan B just in case. I went to class as usual only to return late that evening to an answering machine tape full of messages from men interested in participating in the study. More importantly, what was conveyed in their brief 30-second messages was *relief and validation* that someone out there was acknowledging their struggle.

Upon meeting and interviewing these men, I heard similar themed stories. Most of them had never disclosed to *anyone* that they had an eating disorder. Some men were seeing a therapist for treatment for depression, anxiety, obsessive–compulsive disorder, or a substance abuse problem. However, it was striking that even in the context of this therapy, they had never disclosed their painful experience of their eating disorder. They reported that they felt that the therapist would judge them, assume they were gay, not know how to treat them, or did not want to be a guinea pig, being the first male with an eating disorder they ever treated. This led me into my doctoral studies where I continued researching eating disorders in males and broadened it to men struggling with body dysmorphic disorder (BDD), anabolic steroid users, and compulsive weightlifters. In 2000, I co-wrote a book, *The Adonis Complex* (Pope, Phillips, & Olivardia, 2000), which discussed various manifestations of body image problems in boys and men. And I still get emails from people around the world, including a teenage boy with anorexia in the Midwest, a 40-year-old bulimic New York City businessman, and a primary care physician in Texas who thanked us for writing a book that helped him identify these problems in some of his male patients. In my therapy practice, I treat males of all ages with various eating disorders.

So that is the long response to someone's reaction when I say that I specialize in the treatment of eating disorders in males. But this reaction is an indication that we need more cultural awareness and understanding of this problem. We need more books written that take a closer, more in-depth look at eating disorders, such as anorexia nervosa, in men. Thankfully you hold in your hands that book! Tom Wooldridge took our understanding of anorexia nervosa in males to the next level. He proves that a complex disorder like anorexia in males cannot be understood by a singular framework. The complicated labyrinth of anorexia warrants an entire book to really get it. I am grateful that Tom wrote this book. Its very existence means that men who google "eating disorders in men" will now see this book amongst the very few that have been written for *them*. In the privacy of their own homes, they will echo the same relief and validation that men in my first research study 22 years ago were expressing on my answering machine. More importantly, *Understanding Anorexia Nervosa in Males: An Integrative Approach* is a wonderful resource for clinicians to fully understand the interdisciplinary approach to conceptualization and treatment of these vulnerable patients.

Anorexia nervosa has the highest mortality rate of any psychiatric disorder. One in twenty patients will lose their life to this illness. This is not only due to organ failure and cardiac arrest that severe malnutrition can cause. Twenty percent of deaths related to anorexia are due to suicide. The everyday torture of fighting against your own mind and body becomes too much for some. For those that live with the illness, they are prone to high relapse rates. Given these grim statistics and the lack of information written about males with anorexia, we have two choices. We can simply write this disorder off as too hard to understand and treat in men, or have a call to action to researchers, authors, clinicians, and medical professionals to do their part in raising awareness. I view this book as part of that call to action, by providing the reader with a theoretically sound approach to understanding and treating anorexia nervosa in males. Tom is a researcher, professor, and clinician. As you read through the pages of this book, you will be immersed in research, feel like a student in a class on males with anorexia, and get a sense of what you could do if you were treating a male patient who walks into your office presenting with this condition. I am hopeful that this book spurs other books to be written on the subject.

In 2015, this book is needed. Recently, I conducted a consultation with a severely anorexic 22-year-old male patient who stood six feet tall and weighed 102 pounds. He had a piece of lettuce for breakfast, two carrots for lunch and a tomato with a dash of salt for dinner. He knew he would die if he did not get treatment. He said that he has been suffering with anorexia for years. When he was hospitalized medically, he overheard a nurse telling another nurse, "I could see how a girl could do this, *but a guy?* That is a first." Well, actually it is not a first. Tom can tell you more about that in the first paragraph of Chapter 1. And after that first paragraph, there is a lot more that can be learned. *Understanding Anorexia Nervosa in Males* will teach you.

Roberto Olivardia, PhD, is a Clinical Instructor in the Department of Psychiatry at Harvard Medical School, a Clinical Psychologist in private practice in Lexington, Massachusetts, as well as author of numerous scientific papers and co-author of *The Adonis Complex*, a groundbreaking book about body image problems in men and boys.

References

Pope, H., Phillips, K. & Olivardia, R. (2000). *The Adonis complex: How to identify, treat and prevent body obsession in men and boys.* New York: Simon & Schuster, Inc.

Acknowledgments

Over the years, I've enjoyed reading the acknowledgments section of the books I come across. They're an interesting glimpse into the author's personal life—a bit of the autobiographical in work not intended to be so. Before writing a book, though, I never truly understood how indebted the final product is to patients, colleagues, friends, and family. I can't possibly do justice to that debt here.

I am foremost appreciative of my patients. Our work together is deeply important to me and I am continually moved by your courage. I have learned so much from all of you. I hope that I have done justice to what I've learned in the following pages.

In the writing of this book I drew on the expertise and support of many friends and colleagues, several of whom read and commented on various versions of this manuscript, especially Ken Gladstone, PsyD, Stuart Murray, PhD, Marianne Ault-Riche, LCSW, and Deanna Reardon, PsyD. Throughout the process, my editor, Christopher Teja, was generous with his time and energy, and his confidence in the project kept me moving

I also want to thank two individuals who were pivotal in the writing of this book. Polly Lytle, PhD, spent many hours thinking with me about the feasibility of writing about anorexia nervosa in males and, later, commented on innumerable early drafts. Leigh Cohn, MAT, helped me to become more connected to the world of eating disorders research and treatment. As I wrote, he provided invaluable support, guidance, and practical assistance. Without both of you, this book would have never been written.

My professional home at Golden Gate University provides a launching pad for my clinical work and research pursuits. Through the Nagel T. Miner Research Professorship I was financially supported in writing this book. I am especially fortunate to have such wonderful colleagues who support the Psychology Department. Paul Fouts, PhD, and Marianne Koch, PhD, have both been phenomenally encouraging of my academic work. Frances Sadaya, Cassandra Dilosa, and Nancy Lagomarsino have all helped to keep the Department running during the months I was absorbed in writing.

I am also fortunate to be connected in my professional life to two wonderful organizations. My colleagues at the National Association for Males with Eating Disorders (NAMED) inspire me with their dedication of time, energy, and enthusiasm for this cause. And I am grateful to be a member of the Psychoanalytic Institute of Northern California. From my training cohort and my supervisors, in particular, I have benefitted so much. And while my own analyst will remain anonymous, my gratitude will not.

Finally, my deepest appreciation goes to my family—especially my wife, Caroline Mok, PhD, who is also my colleague. With my nose always in a book, she has had a lot to put up with and I very much appreciate her patient acceptance of my work. Our relationship has been a profound source of learning and fulfillment, and I recognize how lucky I am. My parents, Tom and Luanne, have been deeply supportive and encouraging of my efforts over the years, and for that I am grateful.

With regard to permissions, I wish to thank the journal *Eating Disorders: The Journal of Treatment & Prevention,* in which I published, "An Overview of Anorexia Nervosa in Males" and "A Qualitative Content Analysis of Male Participation in Pro-Anorexia Websites," for allowing me to reproduce aspects of those articles in these chapters.

1   Introduction

In 1689, Richard Morton published his magnum opus, *A Treatise of Consumptions*, which richly describes the many diseases that waste the body's tissues. Although the London physician was recognized at the time for his detailed description of tuberculosis, Morton is known today as the first author to provide a medical account of anorexia nervosa. Ironically, because the disorder is now primarily associated with women and girls, one of the two cases he described is of a 16-year-old adolescent boy. For the boy's "nervous consumption" caused by "sadness and anxious cares" Morton tried a handful of remedies with limited success, eventually advising his patient to retire to the country and adopt a diet of milk and fresh air (Silverman, 1990).

A number of cases were described over the next two centuries. In 1764, for example, Scottish physician Robert Whytt presented a case study of a "lad of 14 years of age" who struggled with "nervous atrophy" and loss of appetite. Around 30 years later, Robert Wilan, English physician and founder of dermatology as a medical specialty, described the death of a young Englishman who abstained from food for 78 days, which the physician attributed to the young man's "mistaken notions in religion" (Silverman, 1990).

Writing in the 1860s, Sir William Gull noted that the illness occurs in male patients. Around the same time, French physician Ernest-Charles Lasgue incisively described the family dynamics of male patients with anorexia nervosa (Andersen, 2014). These two physicians are also known for giving anorexia nervosa its cumbersome name. In fact, the disease received the name "anorexia nervosa" instead of "anorexia hysterica" because of the existence of male patients who could not be labeled "hysterical" according to medical custom at that time (Silverman, 1990). Over the next 100 years, however, males are almost unmentioned in the literature. During this period, the disorder was thought of as a form of post-partum pituitary necrosis, often described in endocrinology textbooks. Of course, this classification excluded males from consideration (Andersen, 2014).

As psychoanalysis gained prominence in the early part of the 20th century, men and boys continued to suffer without recognition or treatment. Early psychoanalytic theories understood anorexia nervosa as a form of conversion hysteria in which the refusal to eat symbolically expressed a repudiation of sexuality, especially fantasies and wishes about oral impregnation. Of course, this excluded males from diagnosis (Swift, 1991). While Arthur Crisp and colleagues notably included males in their empirical studies in the 1960s, until recently males have been excluded from the vast majority of empirical research because of the assumed rarity of the disorder in men. While anorexia nervosa is considered an almost exclusively female disorder, the most recent epidemiological data suggests that as much as 25 percent of the population is male (Hudson, Hiripi, Pope, & Kessler, 2007). And in some ways, the disorder may be more severe in men and boys. When evaluated less than three years after treatment, males with anorexia nervosa are more likely than their female counterparts to have died (Gueguen et al., 2012).

Indeed, men and boys suffering from anorexia nervosa regularly appear in treatment providers' offices. Ken, a 14-year-old boy referred to me by his dentist after the enamel began to chip away on his teeth due to caloric restriction, confides his ongoing questions about sexual orientation and his secret desire to be attractive to his male friends. Jose, in contrast, is immensely enthusiastic about his school's wrestling team and demands absolute perfection from his body. Ray, a 26-year-old man who has struggled with calorie restriction since puberty, mourns a childhood lost to obsessive thinking about food and weight. Each of these boys and men has unique stories to tell, lost potentials to be recaptured, and relationships to be rekindled; fortunately, each has found his way to treatment. In contrast, many men and boys never receive an accurate diagnosis and are overlooked. Others receive treatment only after suffering in silence for many years.

There are a number of reasons that many males with anorexia nervosa are overlooked. Mental health professionals may be less likely to consider the diagnosis in men and boys during differential diagnosis because of its relative scarcity and because of bias in diagnostic criteria. Until the *Diagnostic and Statistical Manual of Mental Disorder, Fifth Edition* (DSM-5), amenorrhea, or the absence of three consecutive menstrual cycles, was a criterion for female anorexia nervosa, though there was no corresponding reproductive hormone-related criterion for men and boys. Although this criterion and its associated diagnostic imbalance was removed in the DSM-5, its unfortunate influence still persists in the minds of treatment providers.

Furthermore, the diagnostic criterion of the DSM-IV that individuals with anorexia nervosa weigh at least 15 percent below the population mean is less appropriate for boys and men. Because males have, on average, half the body fat of females, their weight can be higher – as much as 10 percent below the mean – in spite of active anorexia nervosa (Crisp & Burns, 1990). Put differently, weight, like height, is a bell-shaped curve. A particular boy who is 20 percent above a chosen norm in weight and then loses that 20 percent may have all the signs of anorexia nervosa recognized by an experienced treatment provider but fail to meet DSM-IV criteria (Andersen, 2014). To the benefit of patients and treatment providers, this diagnostic criterion has also been revised in the DSM-5, allowing clinicians to use their own judgment in evaluating "significantly low body weight."

Finally, many men and boys are overlooked because they suffer from subclinical anorexia nervosa or, paradoxically, are suffering from the disorder and because of psychological, familial, or cultural reasons are unaware that they meet the criteria for diagnosis (Räisänen & Hunt, 2014; Raevuori, Keski-Rahkonen, & Hoek, 2014).

Stigma prevents many men and boys from seeking treatment and causes others to seek treatment later in the course of the disorder than they might otherwise. Because of stigma, family, friends, and medical professionals are less likely to recognize the disorder and to encourage help-seeking behavior (Räisänen & Hunt, 2014). Ultimately, males face the double stigma of having a psychiatric disorder and of being a man with a "woman's problem" (Andersen, Cohn, & Holbrook, 2000). In clinical practice, treatment providers see that the widespread perception of eating disorders as afflicting only women and girls prevents men and boys, as well as their families, friends, and medical professionals, from recognizing their symptoms. By the time these suffering males seek treatment the disorder is often deeply entrenched. In one study, male patients emphasized the lack of gender-appropriate information and resources for men as an impediment to seeking treatment (Räisänen & Hunt, 2014). Indeed, males are more likely to seek treatment at a later age than their female counterparts (Gueguen et al., 2012).

Recently, I met with a young man named Josh. As Josh walked into my office with his parents for our first meeting, his thin, fragile body and the dark circles beneath his eyes spoke volumes. The family, I learned, had decided to speak with a mental health provider after Josh's mother found her son's hair, falling away as a result of malnutrition, in the shower drain. When I spoke with his father individually at a later time, he confided, through his tears, that he always thought that only "emotional teenage girls" develop anorexia nervosa. While a number of complex factors prevented the family from seeking treatment earlier, stigma and its cousin, shame, are important ones.

Although there may be more men and boys with anorexia nervosa than epidemiological data suggests, the sex distribution of the disorder is weighted toward girls and women to a degree that is rare among diseases not specifically dependent upon female physiology. With regard to this fact, sociocultural factors are often cited as an explanation for the unequal distribution between the sexes. The intense and destructive cultural and social pressures regarding body weight and shape faced by women in our society have been recognized for some time and are well-documented (Garfinkel & Garner, 1982; Dakanalis & Riva, 2013). Furthermore, the prevalence rates of eating disorders in women have mirrored changes in mass media; as the media ideal has become thinner, the prevalence of anorexia and bulimia nervosa has increased (Harrison & Cantor, 1997). Recently, though, cultural awareness of equally intense pressures on men and boys has been increasing – though certainly not quickly enough (Andersen, Cohn, & Holbrook, 2000). While men have been historically assumed to be immune to media pressures, research shows that they are directly influenced by them (Blond, 2008).

Internalization of a body shape model begins in childhood and peaks during adolescence, when the risk for developing an eating disorder is greatest (Toro, Castro, Gila, & Pombo, 2005). Our body shape model reaches us through many sociocultural avenues such as advertising, television, and diet-related products. Indeed, adolescent boys are increasingly subjected to advertising about dieting, muscular ideals, and even plastic surgery such as pectoral and calf implants (Aubrey, 2006; Calogero, Park, Rahemtulla, & Williams, 2010). And we know that exposure to male bodies in advertisements increases body dissatisfaction in viewers; after exposure to ideal male bodies, viewers report an increased gap between their own muscularity and their ideal (Leit, Gray, & Pope, 2002). In our society, content aimed at men increasingly emphasizes fitness, weight lifting, and muscle toning instead of slimming (Aubrey, 2006). Depictions of men ranging from action toys (Pope, Olivardia, Gruber, & Borowiecki, 1999) to *Playgirl* centerfolds (Leit, Pope, & Gray, 2001) have become strikingly more muscular and lean.

Yet cultural pressures are strikingly different for men and women. As Andersen, Cohn, and Holbrook (2000) wrote, 80 percent of men want to change their weight: 40 percent want to lose weight and 40 percent want to gain weight (p. 56). While this amounts to an enormous percentage of men who are dissatisfied with their bodies, only half of those men want to become thinner, in contrast to women who almost unanimously want to lose weight. The ideal male body widely portrayed in Western society is characterized by a high degree of muscularity and an absence of body adiposity, which is thought to obscure the visibility of one's muscularity (Pope, Phillips, & Olivardia, 2000; Cafri & Thompson, 2004).

Insofar as underlying factors predispose men to eating disorders, these cultural pressures may encourage some men to develop muscle dysmorphia instead of anorexia nervosa (Grieve, 2007). Muscle dysmorphia is a subcategory of body dysmorphic disorder (Pope & Katz, 1994) and, in its diagnostic criteria, shows a number of similarities to anorexia nervosa and often manifests with concomitant symptoms of other eating disorders (Grieve, 2007). Many men who would develop anorexia nervosa under different cultural pressures may more accurately meet the criteria for muscle dysmorphia, which was originally termed "reverse anorexia" (Pope, Katz, & Hudson, 1993).

As I talk with my patient, John, a 16-year-old male with anorexia nervosa and an aspiring athlete, I am struck by his idealization of a muscular male body. When I ask about bodies that he particularly admires, he begins to talk about his favorite film, *The Machinist*, and how Christian Bale's "thin and ripped" physique is an object of particular admiration. I raise the contradiction of John's idealization of a "thin and ripped" physique with his own pursuit of starvation and he responds immediately, "But when I eat, the food goes straight to my stomach. Even when I lift weights and exercise! Most of all, I want to be muscular, but if I can't have that, it's better to be skinny than fat."

Although there are many factors at play here, I agree with John's verdict that the physique he aspires to is likely inaccessible. Indeed, many male images portrayed in the media may not even be attainable without drugs like anabolic steroids (Kouri, Pope, Katz, & Oliva, 1995; Pope, Phillips, & Olivardia, 2000), not to mention obsessive regimens of exercise and diet. Although the relationship between muscle dysmorphia and anorexia nervosa is complex, what is clear is that the increasingly impossible ideal male body promulgated by the media directly impacts body dissatisfaction (Grieve, 2007).

Another explanation for the skewed sex distribution of anorexia nervosa is that the role of fat development in puberty and what it entails for gender roles is different in boys and girls. In girls' puberty, fat increases more than muscle. The development of breasts is followed by an increase in hip size and subcutaneous fat deposits on the buttocks, abdomen, and thighs. Boys, on the other hand, experience a marked development of muscle relative to fat. Because increase in fat is a less pronounced part of boys' progress through puberty, they may be less likely to become preoccupied with it.

There are some factors that contribute to the development of anorexia nervosa in men and boys that may be less notable in women and girls. One of the factors emphasized in male anorexia nervosa is marked anxiety about sexual activities and relationships (Herzog, Bradburn, & Newman, 1990). In fact, males with anorexia nervosa have significantly more sexual anxiety than females with the disorder (Fitcher & Daser, 1987) and males with anorexia nervosa are often asexual. In one study, adolescent boys with anorexia nervosa were significantly less likely to have had pre-morbid sexual encounters than adolescent girls with anorexia nervosa (Herzog, Norman, Gordon, & Pepose, 1984). Also, the chances that a boy or man with the disorder will recover successfully increases with the frequency of his pre-morbid sexual activity (Burns & Crisp, 1985). Furthermore, as sexual drive is reduced through starvation, sexual conflict may be temporarily resolved. Some have speculated that reducing sexual conflict may play a role in the genesis or maintenance of anorexia nervosa in males (Crisp, 1983). Throughout the book, we will explore the implications of these findings.

Another factor is that males with anorexia nervosa often have a history of weight-related teasing (Andersen, Cohn, & Holbrook, 2000). Indeed, clinical experience suggests that peer criticism about weight is a precipitant factor in a large number of cases. In my clinical practice, I regularly hear from young men struggling with a range of problems, from eating disorders to run-of-the-mill questions about their developing bodies, who describe the agony of being teased and taunted about their appearance. In addition to being intensely traumatic and shameful, these experiences also increase weight concern and body dissatisfaction, which are risk factors for the development of eating disorders.

A final factor is that men and boys with anorexia nervosa tend to be in different subsets of the population than their female counterparts (Wooldridge & Lytle, 2012). Although anorexia nervosa is associated with models and ballet dancers, the disorder in men and boys more often occurs in sports that require weight control, such as jockeys, wrestlers, and swimmers (Andersen, Cohn, & Holbrook, 2000). With their emphasis on "making weight," these sports increase the risk that their participants will develop anorexia nervosa. In addition, anorexia nervosa in males also has an increased incidence in the homosexual population (Feldman & Meyer, 2007). In fact, boys and men with anorexia nervosa see themselves and are seen by others as more feminine than other males (Fitcher & Daser, 1987). No corresponding disparity has been found in females. These observations and their implications are discussed at greater length in Chapter 6: The Culture and Gender Metaframework, where we explore cultural factors related to anorexia nervosa in men and boys.

With these and other differences between anorexia nervosa in males and females, it is essential that we have a comprehensive understanding of the disorder as it manifests in men and boys. In this book, we develop an integrative model of anorexia nervosa in males. Drawing from Pinsof's (1995, 2005) integrative problem-centered therapy, we account for biological, systemic, cultural, psychodynamic, and spiritual perspectives on the disorder, highlighting the ways that it manifests in males differently than in females. And because integrative problem-centered therapy organizes information from multiple domains into a single, unified understanding of how to solve the presenting problem, this model provides a truly comprehensive formulation and treatment approach.

An integrative formulation is essential because many existing explanations for anorexia nervosa emphasize a single etiological factor and, thus, produce treatments that are unable to address the global nature of the disorder. If we believe anorexia nervosa results from a specific family dynamic, for example, our treatment will address that family dynamic while neglecting factors such gender identity, nutrition, and neurochemistry. An integrative model brings together available knowledge in order to address anorexia nervosa as a holistic phenomenon (Andersen, 1990).

In addition to promoting more efficacious treatment, developing a comprehensive understanding speaks to the stigma and misunderstanding so prevalent for men and boys with anorexia nervosa. Indeed, stigma is deeply intertwined with the experience of the illness and all too frequently interferes with seeking treatment. Because anorexia nervosa is thought of as a "woman's problem," many men and boys' symptoms are not recognized and addressed with appropriate treatment (Räisänen & Hunt, 2014).

An integrative understanding recognizes that bringing order to the experience of an illness by developing a narrative consistent with our experience of it is an important part of healing. Kleinman (1988) began with the premise that witnessing and ordering the experience of illness can be therapeutic. White and Epston (1990) went further and said that the performance of our stories creates our lives and relationships.

> In striving to make sense of life, persons face the task of arranging their experiences of events … across time in such a way as to arrive at a coherent account of themselves and the world around them … This account can be referred to as a story or self-narrative. The success of this storying of experience provides persons with a sense of continuity and meaning in their lives, and this is relied upon for the ordering of daily lives and for the interpretation of further experiences.
>
> (White & Epston, 1990, p. 10)

Stories that capture the complexity of our lives reveal the possibilities for healing available. Problems arise when our stories do not sufficiently represent our lived experience. An inadequate narrative of anorexia nervosa makes recovery more difficult (Garrett, 1998). Thus, revising simplistic or limited stories is an essential component of recovery. In recent years, clinicians increasingly hear men and boys say they are embarrassed to suffer from a "female problem" like anorexia nervosa. However, as Andersen, Cohn, and Holbrook (2000) wrote, "Few thought other men obsessively counted calories, were preoccupied with their weight, or binged and purged. Contrary to popular belief, millions of men face such personal struggles" (p. 26). Because males inherit an understanding of anorexia nervosa as a "woman's problem," confusion and alienation accompany their efforts toward change.

This book, then, develops an integrative approach to the formulation and treatment of anorexia nervosa in men and boys. In the second chapter, we provide an overview of existing approaches to the treatment of anorexia nervosa, focusing specifically on cognitive-behavioral therapy (Pike, Carter, & Olmsted, 2010), specialist supportive clinical management (McIntosh, Jordan, & Bulik, 2010), cognitive remediation

(Tchanturia & Hambrook, 2010), family-based treatments (Eisler, Lock, & le Grange, 2010), psychodynamic treatments (Zerbe, 2010), dialectical behavior therapy (Linehan, 1993), and acceptance and commitment therapy (Hayes, Strosahl, & Wilson, 2011). We also review additional components of treatment such as pharmacotherapy (Kaplan & Howlett, 2010), nutritional rehabilitation (Rock, 2010), and intensive multidisciplinary approaches like inpatient and day hospital treatment (Olmsted et al., 2010). We lay out the reasons that another approach – an integrative approach tailored to men and boys – is warranted. In addition, we provide an overview of Pinsof's (1995, 2005) integrative problem-centered therapy, which is the model upon which this book's approach is based, and unpack its key terms and orienting concepts – metaframework, constraint, patient system, and problem-maintenance space.

In the third chapter, we provide an overview of the process of assessment and diagnosis, with special consideration to the problems faced by men and boys with anorexia nervosa. In addition, we discuss difficulties encountered by patients in making contact with a treatment provider and the essential and often difficult process of forming a working alliance. In discussing these difficulties, we highlight the importance of working with ambivalence in the early stages of treatment, acknowledge the difficulties posed by stigma to treatment engagement, and explore the obstructive nature of traditional constructions of masculinity on help-seeking behavior.

In Chapters 4 through 9, we develop the five metaframeworks (Breunlin, Schwartz, & Mac Kune-Karrer, 1992; Pinsof, 1995, 2005) that comprise our approach: systemic, biological, cultural, psychodynamic, and spiritual. In the seventh chapter, we focus specifically on a new frontier of investigation regarding anorexia nervosa in men and boys – pro-anorexia Internet forums, which are increasingly appearing in the treatment situation. Each is these metaframeworks is developed by integrating diverse areas of research and clinical experience into a more unified understanding. In the tenth and final chapter, we describe the clinical application of our model and illustrate this process with a complex clinical case.

References

Andersen, A. (2014). A brief history of eating disorders in males. In L. Cohn & R. Lemberg (Eds.), *Current findings on males with eating disorders* (pp. 4–10). New York: Routledge.

Andersen, A. E. (1990). Diagnosis and treatment of males with eating disorders. In A. E. Andersen (Ed.), *Males with Eating Disorders* (pp. 133–162). New York: Brunner/Mazel, Inc.

Andersen, A. E., Cohn, L., & Holbrook, T. (2000). *Making weight: Healing men's conflicts with food, weight, and shape*. Carlsbad, CA: Gürze Books.

Aubrey, J. S. (2006). Effects of sexually objectifying media on self-objectification and body surveillance in undergraduates: Results of a 2-year panel study. *Journal of Communication, 56*, 366–386.

Blond, A. (2008). Impact of exposure to images of ideal bodies on male body dissatisfaction: A review. *Body Image, 5*(3), 244–250.

Breunlin, D., Schwartz, R., & Mac Kune-Karrer, B. (1992). *Metaframeworks: Transcending the models of family therapy.* San Francisco, CA: Jossey-Bass.

Burns, T. & Crisp, A. H. (1985). Factors affecting prognosis in male anorexics. *Journal of Psychiatric Research, 19,* 323–328.

Cafri, G. & Thompson, J. K. (2004). Measuring male body image: A review of the current methodology. *Psychology of Men and Masculinity, 5,* 18–29.

Calogero, R. M., Park, L. E., Rahemtulla, Z. K., & Williams, K. C. D. (2010). Predicting excessive body image concerns among British university students: The unique role of appearance-based rejection sensitivity. *Body Image, 7,* 78–81.

Crisp, A. H. (1983). Some aspects of the psychopathology of anorexia nervosa. In P. L. Darby, P. E. Garfinkel, D. M. Garner, & D. C. Coscina (Eds.), *Anorexia nervosa: Recent developments in research* (pp. 15–28). New York: Alan Liss.

Crisp, A. H. & Burns, T. (1990). Primary anorexia nervosa in the male and female: A comparison of clinical features and prognosis. In A. E. Andersen (Ed.), *Males with eating disorders* (pp. 77–99). New York: Brunner/Mazel.

Dakanalis, A. & Riva, G. (2013). Current considerations for eating and body-related disorders among men. In L. B. Sams & J. A. Keels (Eds.), *Handbook on body image: Gender differences, sociocultural influences and health implications* (pp. 195–216). New York: Nova Science Publishers.

Eisler, I., Lock, J., & le Grange, D. (2010). Family based treatments for adolescents with anorexia nervosa: Single-family and multi-family approaches. In C. M. Grilo & J. E. Mitchell (Eds.), *The treatment of eating disorders: A clinical handbook* (pp. 150–174). New York: The Guilford Press.

Feldman, M. B. & Meyer, I. H. (2007). Childhood abuse and eating disorders in gay and bisexual men. *International Journal of Eating Disorders, 40*(5), 418–423.

Fitcher, M. M. & Daser, C. (1987). Symptomatology, psychosexual development, and gender identity in 42 anorexic males. *Psychological Medicine, 17,* 409–418.

Garfinkel, P. E. & Garner, D. M. (1982). *Anorexia nervosa: A multidimensional perspective.* New York: Brunner/Mazel.

Garrett, C. (1998). *Beyond anorexia: Narrative, spirituality, and recovery.* Cambridge: Cambridge University Press.

Grieve, F. G. (2007). A conceptual model of factors contributing to the development of muscle dysmorphia. *Eating Disorders, 15*(1), 63–80.

Gueguen, J., Godart, N., Chambry, J., Brun-Eberentz, A., Foulon, C., Snezana, M., ... & Huas, C. (2012). Severe anorexia nervosa in men: Comparison with severe AN in women and analysis of mortality. *International Journal of Eating Disorders, 45*(4), 537–545.

Harrison, K. & Cantor, J. (1997). The relationship between media consumption and eating disorders. *Journal of Communication, 47,* 40–67.

Hayes, S. C., Strosahl, K. D., & Wilson, K. G. (2011). *Acceptance and commitment therapy: The process and practice of mindful change.* New York: Guilford Press.

Herzog, D. B., Bradburn, I. S., & Newman, K. (1990). Sexuality in males with eating disorders. In A. E. Andersen (Ed.), *Males with eating disorders* (pp. 40–53). New York: Brunner/Mazel.

Herzog, D. B., Norman, D. K., Gordon, C., & Pepose, M. (1984). Sexual conflict and eating disorders in 27 males. *American Journal of Psychiatry*, *141*, 989–990.

Hudson, J., Hiripi, E., Pope, H., & Kessler, R. (2007). The prevalence and correlates of eating disorders in the National Comorbidity Survey Replication. *Biological Psychiatry, 61*(3), 348–358.

Kaplan, A. S. & Howlett, A. (2010). Pharmacotherapy for anorexia nervosa. In C. M. Grilo & J. E. Mitchell (Eds.), *The treatment of eating disorders: A clinical handbook* (pp. 175–186). New York: The Guilford Press.

Kleinman, A. (1988). *The illness narratives: Suffering, healing, and the human condition*. New York: Basic Books.

Kouri, E. M., Pope Jr., H. G., Katz, D. L., & Oliva, P. (1995). Fat-free mass index in users and nonusers of anabolic-androgenic steroids. *Clinical Journal of Sport Medicine, 5*(4), 223–228.

Leit, R. A., Gray, J. J., & Pope, H. G. (2002). The media's representation of the ideal male body: A cause for muscle dysmorphia? *International Journal of Eating Disorders, 31*(3), 334–338.

Leit, R. A., Pope, H. G., & Gray, J. J. (2001). Cultural expectations of muscularity in men: The evolution of Playgirl centerfolds. *International Journal of Eating Disorders, 29*(1), 90–93.

Linehan, M. (1993). *Cognitive-behavioral treatment of borderline personality disorder*. New York: Guilford Press.

McIntosh, V. V. W., Jordan, J., & Bulik, C. M. (2010). Specialist supportive clinical management for anorexia nervosa. In C. M. Grilo & J. E. Mitchell (Eds.), *The treatment of eating disorders: A clinical handbook* (pp. 150–174). New York: The Guilford Press.

Olmsted, M. P., McFarlane, T. L., Carter, J. C., Trottier, K., Woodside, D. B., & Dimitropoulos, G. (2010). Inpatient and day hospital treatment for anorexia nervosa. In C. M. Grilo, & J. E. Mitchell (Eds.), *The treatment of eating disorders: A clinical handbook* (pp. 198–211). New York: The Guilford Press.

Pike, K. M., Carter, J. C., & Olmsted, M. P. (2010). Cognitive-behavioral therapy for anorexia nervosa. In C. M. Grilo & J. E. Mitchell (Eds.), *The treatment of eating disorders: A clinical handbook* (pp. 83–107). New York: The Guilford Press.

Pinsof, W. M. (1995). *Integrative problem-centered therapy: A synthesis of family, individual, and biological therapies*. New York: Basic Books.

Pinsof, W. M. (2005). Integrative problem-centered therapy. In J. C. Norcross & M. R. Goldfried (Eds.), *Handbook of psychotherapy integration* (pp. 282–402). Oxford: Oxford University Press.

Pope, H. G. & Katz, D. L. (1994). Psychiatric and medical effects of anabolic-androgenic steroid use: A controlled study of 160 athletes. *Archives of General Psychiatry, 51*(5), 375–382.

Pope, H. G., Katz, D. L., & Hudson, J. I. (1993). Anorexia nervosa and "reverse anorexia" among 108 male bodybuilders. *Comprehensive Psychiatry, 34*(6), 406–409.

Pope, H. G., Olivardia, R., Gruber, A., & Borowiecki, J. (1999). Evolving ideals of male body image as seen through action toys. *International Journal of Eating Disorders, 26*(1), 65–72.

Pope, H. G., Phillips, K. A., & Olivardia, R. (2000). *The Adonis complex: How to identify, treat, and prevent body obsession in men and boys*. New York: Touchstone.

Raevuori, A., Keski-Rahkonen, A., & Hoek, H. W. (2014). A review of eating disorders in males. *Current Opinion in Psychiatry, 27*(6), 426–430.

Räisänen, U. & Hunt, K. (2014). The role of gendered constructions of eating disorders in delayed help-seeking in men: A qualitative interview study. *British Medical Journal Open, 4*(4) e004342, doi:10.1136/bmjopen-2013-004342

Rock, C. L. (2010). Nutritional rehabilitation for anorexia nervosa. In C. M. Grilo & J. E. Mitchell (Eds.), *The treatment of eating disorders: A clinical handbook* (pp. 187–197). New York: The Guilford Press.

Silverman, J. A. (1990). Anorexia nervosa in the male: Early historic cases. In A. E. Andersen (Ed.), *Males with eating disorders* (pp. 3–8). New York: Brunner/Mazel.

Swift, W. J. (1991). Bruch revisited: The role of interpretation of transference and resistance in the psychotherapy of eating disorders. In C. Johnson (Ed.), *Psychodynamic treatment of anorexia nervosa and bulimia* (pp. 51–67). New York: The Guilford Press.

Tchanturia, K. & Hambrook, D. (2010). Cognitive remediation therapy for anorexia nervosa. In C. M. Grilo & J. E. Mitchell (Eds.), *The treatment of eating disorders: A clinical handbook* (pp. 130–150). New York: The Guilford Press.

Toro, J., Castro, J., Gila, A., & Pombo, C. (2005). Assessment of sociocultural influences on the body shape model in adolescent males with anorexia nervosa. *European Eating Disorders Review, 13*, 351–359.

White, M. & Epston, D. (1990). *Narrative means to therapeutic ends.* New York: Norton.

Wooldridge, T. & Lytle, P. (2012). An overview of anorexia nervosa in males. *Eating Disorders: Journal of Treatment & Prevention, 20*(5), 368–378.

Zerbe, K. J. (2010). Psychodynamic therapy for eating disorders. In C. M. Grilo & J. E. Mitchell (Eds.), *The treatment of eating disorders: A clinical handbook* (pp. 339–358). New York: The Guilford Press.

2   An Integrative Approach

In this chapter, we begin with an exploration of existing approaches to the treatment of anorexia nervosa including cognitive-behavioral therapy, specialist supportive clinical management, cognitive remediation, family-based treatments, psychodynamic treatments, and third-wave approaches such as mindfulness and acceptance and commitment therapy. We also review the adjunctive interventions of pharmacotherapy, nutritional rehabilitation, inpatient and day hospital treatment, and psychoeducation. Each of these modalities has immense value for our understanding of anorexia nervosa in both males and females. In the integrative model proposed in this book, we incorporate many of their findings and techniques to address the whole of the male patient with anorexia nervosa.

After providing an overview of these modalities as well as the empirical research supporting them, we discuss the model developed in this book, which is adapted from Pinsof's (1995, 2005) integrative problem-centered therapy. In this discussion, we attend to the model's foundational concepts and theoretical structure as well as how the model will be used to develop a more comprehensive understanding and approach to anorexia nervosa in men and boys. Finally, we propose a way of thinking about the therapeutic alliance, a core component of effective intervention, which is integral to the model as implemented in clinical practice with boys and men with anorexia nervosa.

Existing Approaches

At present, a number of treatment approaches for anorexia nervosa have been outlined and researched, though there is not firm consensus on the best approach to treatment. Broadly, these approaches include cognitive-behavioral therapy (Pike, Carter, & Olmsted, 2010), specialist supportive clinical management (McIntosh, Jordan, & Bulik, 2010), cognitive remediation (Tchanturia & Hambrook, 2010), family-based treatments (Eisler, Lock, & le Grange, 2010), psychodynamic treatments (Zerbe, 2010), dialectical behavior therapy (Linehan, 1993), and acceptance and commitment therapy (Hayes, Strosahl, & Wilson, 2011). Additional components of treatment include pharmacotherapy (Kaplan & Howlett, 2010), nutritional rehabilitation (Rock, 2010), intensive multidisciplinary approaches like inpatient and day hospital treatment (Olmsted et al., 2010), and psychoeducation (Garner, 1997).

Cognitive-behavioral therapy (CBT) has a reputation as one of the most influential and well-validated models of psychotherapy for a wide range of psychiatric disorders (Nathan & Gorman, 2002). CBT for anorexia nervosa has been developed by a number of researchers and clinicians (see Pike, Carter, & Olmsted, 2010 for an overview). Yet in contrast to other eating disorders, such as bulimia nervosa, CBT is notable for its lack of empirical validation for the treatment of anorexia nervosa (Garner, Vitousek, & Pike, 1997). In recent years, a new "enhanced" form of cognitive-behavioral therapy (CBT-E) has been gaining empirical validation for the treatment of anorexia nervosa (Fairburn et al., 2013).

In its earliest development, cognitive conceptualizations of anorexia nervosa recognized that abnormal attitudes toward food and weight were persistent features of the disorder and interfered with full recovery; indeed, these attitudes were found to persist even after recovery of normal body weight (Dally & Gomez, 1979). At present, cognitive-behavioral treatment for anorexia nervosa encompasses cognitive restructuring to address characteristic attitudes about body weight and shape, education about relevant topics such as normal eating patterns, symptoms of malnutrition, maintaining healthy body weight, and binge/purge behavior, and, finally, behavioral interventions to address problematic behaviors such as binge/purge symptoms (Garner, Vitousek, & Pike, 1997).

Specialist supportive clinical management for anorexia nervosa is an outpatient treatment that addresses core symptoms of anorexia nervosa, including low weight, restrictive eating, and compensatory behaviors. It combines features of clinical management and supportive psychotherapy. In this context, clinical management refers to good clinical care from an experienced clinician but without a specific treatment regimen. Supportive psychotherapy includes techniques such as conveying support and acceptance, working collaboratively toward change, and communicating optimism about healing (see McIntosh, Jordan, & Bulik, 2010 for an excellent overview of this modality).

Cognitive remediation attempts to address the process rather than the content of thinking, thus helping patients with anorexia nervosa to gain increased awareness of their own thinking style. This intervention is an intensive training component of the Maudsley model of family-based therapy discussed below. For example, research suggests that patients with anorexia nervosa demonstrate an extreme focus on details at the expense of global processing, which, for example, can manifest as a disabling attention to food and calories. Similarly, patients often demonstrate marked cognitive inflexibility, manifesting as highly rigid behavior in many aspects of their day-to-day lives. By helping to shift aspects of thinking styles that are problematic through learning tasks and self-reflection, patients with anorexia nervosa can develop new strategies for thinking and living (see Tchanturia & Hambrook, 2010 for an overview).

Family-based treatments (FBTs) have a long history in the treatment of anorexia nervosa, especially with younger patients. Based on the treatment model developed at the Maudsley Hospital in the 1980s, family-based treatment has a strong evidence base and, viewing the parents as an immense resource in the child's recovery, focuses on helping parents to learn the behavioral and psychological strategies to help their child toward weight restoration (see Eisler, Lock, & le Grange, 2010 for an overview). Indeed, family-based treatment has much to recommend it, including the fact that it is a collaborative model that empowers, instead of stigmatizes, suffering families. From a theoretical perspective, family-based treatment suggests that there is a lack of obvious family etiology for anorexia nervosa and, if there are risk factors, they lack the force of an explanatory mechanism and instead are nonspecific, increasing the risk for a wide range of psychological disorders (Eisler, 1995). Family-based treatment is discussed at greater length in Chapter 4: The Systemic Metaframework.

Psychodynamic approaches to treatment are singularly notable for their long history in the treatment of eating disorders and for their emphasis on patients' personal narratives and subjective experiences. Psychodynamic psychotherapy aims to explore and modify the intrapsychic and interpersonal issues that relate to the patient's struggle with anorexia nervosa, many of which manifest themselves in the relationship between patient and clinician. At the conclusion of treatment, patients have developed an understanding of the (often unconscious) factors that contributed to their eating disorder and discovered more effective ways of negotiating interpersonal relationships and managing difficult emotions (see Zerbe, 2010 for an overview). Psychodynamic approaches are discussed at greater length in Chapter 8: The Psychodynamic Metaframework.

Dialectical behavior therapy (DBT) was originally developed to treat patients with borderline personality disorder (Linehan, 1993). Emphasizing the dialectic between acceptance and change, dialectical behavior therapy provides skills training (mindfulness, distress tolerance, interpersonal effectiveness, and emotion regulation) through a combination of individual and group therapy as well as phone coaching. In addition, clinicians receive support through participation in a therapist consultation team. With modifications such as highlighting eating disordered behaviors as well as teaching nutrition skills, dialectical behavior therapy may be appropriate for the treatment of eating disorders (Wisniewski & Kelly, 2003). In early research, dialectical behavior therapy appears promising for the treatment of anorexia nervosa (Salbach, Klinkowski, Pfeiffer, Lehmkuhl, & Korte, 2007).

Acceptance and commitment therapy (ACT) is a cognitive-behavioral treatment that targets experiential avoidance, or the unwillingness to accept negative thoughts, feelings, and emotions, and ineffective attempts to control these experiences. According to acceptance and commitment therapy, negative thoughts, feelings, and emotions may or may not produce behavior problems. Avoidance of these experiences, however, undermines pursuit of valued behavior (Hayes, Strosahl, & Wilson, 2011). At present, case reports have been published describing the application of acceptance and commitment therapy to the treatment of anorexia nervosa (Heffner, Sperry, Eifert, & Detweiler, 2002) as well as to patients with a history of treatment for anorexia nervosa (Berman, Boutelle, & Crow, 2009).

Pharmacotherapy is an essential adjunct to the multidisciplinary treatment of anorexia nervosa (Kaplan & Howlett, 2010). Indeed, multiple systems of neurotransmitters, such as serotonin and dopamine, are intertwined with appetite and eating (Bosanac, Norman, Burrows, & Beumont, 2005). At present, empirical evidence for medication treatment is lacking and the Food and Drug Administration has not approved any specific medication for the treatment of anorexia nervosa (Kaplan & Howlett, 2010). In spite of this, the majority of patients with anorexia nervosa receive medication treatment to address comorbid conditions, to facilitate eating through anxiety reduction, and to effect appetite and weight (Rossi et al., 2007).

Nutritional rehabilitation is essential for weight restoration and improved nutritional status in patients who have suffered from malnutrition (Rock, 2010). While nutritional rehabilitation is not commensurate with psychological recovery, it promotes restoration of the metabolic system, addresses medical complications, and promotes a level of cognitive functioning required for effective psychological work to take place. Because overly aggressive refeeding and inadequate monitoring can have serious consequences, nutritional rehabilitation is best approached through adjunctive treatment; however, psychological interventions should address the intense conflict patients with anorexia nervosa experience as weight restoration proceeds.

Patients with moderate to severe anorexia nervosa often receive higher levels of care, such as inpatient care and day hospital treatment (Olmsted et al., 2010). At present, there are no universally agreed upon criteria for identifying patients most appropriate for these more intensive forms of treatment. Furthermore, third-party payers are continually cutting funding for inpatient care for psychiatric disorders and eating disorders in particular (Andersen, Bowers, & Evans, 1997). In spite of these factors, because of the entrenched and life-threatening nature of anorexia nervosa at more severe stages of the illness, the comprehensive attention provided by these forms of treatment is often necessary.

The goal of *inpatient hospital treatment* for anorexia nervosa is to achieve speedy short-term improvement and to prepare patients for transition to a less intense, stepped-down partial hospital treatment, followed by long-term outpatient care. Admission to inpatient treatment is a clinical decision based on multiple factors, with the most common reasons being severe or rapid weight loss, lack of response to outpatient treatment, significant psychiatric comorbidity, medical complications, the lack of outpatient facilities or a treatment-compromising psychosocial environment, or, most often, some combination of these factors (see Andersen, Bowers, & Evans, 1997 for an overview).

Partial or day hospitalization programs are a means of providing a higher level of care than outpatient treatment without the financial costs of inpatient treatment. The goals of these programs include reducing symptomatic behaviors, nutritional rehabilitation, and the identification of psychological and familial dynamics that contribute to each patient's eating disorder. While the theoretical approaches differ in each program, typically a combination of biological, psychological, familial, and sociocultural interventions are provided (see Kaplan & Olmsted, 1997 for an overview).

Finally, *psychoeducational principles* are woven throughout most forms of treatment for anorexia nervosa. Indeed, it is well-recognized that specific information in several areas is essential in the process of recovery. Patients with eating disorders suffer from misconceptions about factors that cause and maintain symptoms, including the multiple causes of disordered eating, the set-point theory of body weight, the effects of starvation on behavior, the principles of restoring regular eating, the problems with vomiting, laxative, and diuretic use, determining a healthy body weight, potential physical complications, and relapse prevention techniques (Garner, 1997).

An Integrative Approach

With a number of approaches to treatment, each with its unique strengths and accompanying base of research, why propose yet another approach? First, the integrative approach to anorexia nervosa in males developed in this book recognizes that each of these approaches contains significant clinical wisdom and utility. As we will see, the practicing clinician, depending on that particular clinician's training and experience, may utilize theories and interventions from each of these models and may also coordinate with providers who specialize in other treatment modalities, whether pharmacotherapy, family therapy, or nutritional rehabilitation.

Second, in approaching patients with eating disorders, the average clinician rarely implements strictly manualized treatment protocols; indeed, respecting the consequential uniqueness (Hoffman, 2009) of each patient, therapists in the trenches of outpatient treatment make use of a wide range of understandings and diverse interventions in helping their patients move toward health. Third, while each of the treatments previously outlined has its strengths, each also neglects important aspects of the patient's experience – whether biological, cultural, familial, psychodynamic, or spiritual. Because of this, a multidisciplinary and integrative approach is required to address the whole patient.

Finally, men and boys with anorexia nervosa present with a unique clinical picture when compared to their female counterparts (Wooldridge & Lytle, 2012). Men and boys, for example, encounter a different kind of stigma (Räisänen & Hunt, 2014) and alienation (Wooldridge, 2014) than do women and girls. Researchers and clinicians have previously suggested that while men and boys may not need entirely new forms of treatment, they do need treatment approaches that are specifically tailored to them (Greenberg & Schoen, 2008; Wooldridge & Lytle, 2012). Because stigma and alienation are central to the experience of anorexia nervosa in men and boys, for example, they must be accounted for in both the delivery and implementation of treatment. In line with these differences, the model developed in this book focuses on the *male* experience of anorexia nervosa.

We adapt integrative problem-centered therapy (Pinsof, 1995, 2005) to organize our thinking. Integrative problem-centered therapy provides a way to organize information from research in multiple areas of psychology about a presenting problem into a single, unified understanding of how to solve that problem. This model requires the introduction of several key concepts. The first is the *patient system*. In integrative problem-centered therapy, the patient system contains all the human systems (biological, psychological, social) involved in the maintenance or resolution of the client's presenting problem.

In other words, who is the patient? As it turns out, every problem has its own, unique patient system. In contrast to many existing therapies that preemptively specify who the patient is, in this model the patient system has to be discovered. And insofar as a human system affects the maintenance or resolution of the presenting problem, it is part of the patient system. (In contrast, factors that contributed to the genesis of the problem but no longer constrain its resolution are not included in the patient system, though they may be a topic of discussion in exploratory interventions designed to elucidate psychodynamic themes and to promote self-understanding.)

Of course, the patient system will be much larger than the systems directly involved in psychotherapeutic intervention. Pinsof (1995) distinguishes between the *direct system*, which is comprised of those subsystems that are directly involved in treatment at any particular time, and the *indirect system*, which contains subsystems that are not directly involved in treatment at any particular time. Throughout the course of treatment, members of the patient system may move into the direct system and vice versa.

Jay Goodstone (a pseudonym, as are all patient names in this book), a 14-year-old boy who was referred to me by his dentist after the enamel began to chip away on his teeth, arrives with his parents, Kit and Joseph.

Patient system	
Direct patient system Jay Goodstone (identified patient) Kit Goodstone Joseph Goodstone	**Indirect patient system**

Figure 2.1 Goodstone family patient system

Source: Adapted from Pinsof (1995)

At the beginning of our first meeting, the direct patient system consisted of the three members of the Goodstone family; the indirect patient system consists only of their dentist, who has not yet become actively involved in the intervention process. The patient system, with its divisions of direct and indirect patient systems, is illustrated in Figure 2.1. Because of Jay's strikingly low body weight, intervention may begin with FBT, which includes the parental subsystem, to actively focus on some degree of weight restoration. When enough weight has been regained to ensure medical stability, the parents may recede into the indirect system for a period of time as more exploratory and meaning making interventions are deployed.

The notion of *metaframeworks* is central to integrative problem-centered therapy (Breunlin, Schwartz, & Mac Kune-Karrer, 1997). Metaframeworks replace specific theories of problem formation and maintenance and, instead, attempt to extract and organize the most common, systemic, and generic components of each of these models (Breunlin, Pinsof, Russell, & Lebow, 2011). In this model, each metaframework integrates diverse theoretical approaches to understanding and intervening in a particular domain of human functioning or activity. For example, the family systems metaframework integrates a wide range of theories of good enough family functioning such as structural family therapy's approach to the treatment of eating disorders (Fishman, 2004), FBTs for anorexia nervosa (Eisler, Lock, & le Grange, 2010), and empirical research on families with an anorexic member who is male. In integrating this research, we highlight issues that are particularly relevant to men and boys with anorexia nervosa.

The second idea is the theory of *constraints*, which says, "people do what they do or think what they think because they are prevented (that is, constrained) from doing or thinking something else" (Breunlin, 1999). The idea is derived from Bateson's (1972) notion of negative (in contrast to positive) explanation, which casts intervention as a task of identification and removal of obstacles to problem solving. Ultimately, positive and negative explanations are two sides of the same coin. However, an emphasis on lifting constraints to problem resolution casts the task of therapy as a problem-solving enterprise and, instead of focusing on patient's deficits, emphasizes their strengths. Arguably, this approach also elicits less resistance in patients (Breunlin, 1999).

In this way of thinking, each patient system is prevented from solving the presenting problem by a unique web of constraints that keeps the problem in place. For example, a therapist interested in positive explanation might ask, "Why does Jay starve himself to the point of physical danger?" The therapist interested in negative explanation, on the other hand, would ask, "What keeps Jay from eating a healthy and balanced diet?"

The theory of constraints posits no causal explanation for why the problem is in place. Instead, the theory recognizes that when a human system is repeatedly unable to solve a problem, that system becomes stuck. In this state, members of the system are more likely to engage in problem-maintaining behaviors and, thus, it is unlikely that novel ideas or behaviors will appear. In other words, the problem continues to exist because the human system is constrained from finding a solution (Breunlin, 1999).

Finally, the *problem-maintenance space* helps to visualize the presenting problem within the patient system. As shown in Figure 2.2, the problem-maintenance space is a set of five levels.[1] Each level represents a domain of activity and contains a metaframework for that domain as well as a set of constraints within that domain (Pinsof, 1995).

In the following chapters, we develop a metaframework for each level of the revised problem-maintenance space. First, the *systemic* level of the problem-maintenance space recognizes that the problem lies in the patient system instead of in the individual client. It recognizes that constraints can exist in how the patient system organizes and conducts itself with regard to the presenting problem and also that this problem can be transmitted through the generations (Pinsof, 1995). Second, the *biological* level of the problem-maintenance space recognizes that biological symptoms – whether severe malnutrition or endocrine abnormalities – may constrain problem resolution.

Systemic
Biological
Culture and gender
Psychodynamic
Spiritual

Figure 2.2 Five levels of the problem-maintenance space

Source: Adapted from Pinsof (1995)

Third, the *culture and gender* level of the problem-maintenance space recognizes that all members of the patient system exist in a wide array of contexts including ethnicity, race, religion, class, sexual preference, and many more. In line with this, gender is a notion that is both socially constructed and biologically determined. Each of these contexts may specify both normative beliefs and behaviors (Breunlin, Pinsof, Russell, & Lebow, 2011). Both culture and gender are intimately intertwined with the experience of anorexia nervosa in men and boys and may constrain its resolution – for example, normative beliefs about masculinity may make it more difficult for men and boys to engage and continue in the treatment process.

Fourth, the *psychodynamic* level of the problem-maintenance space recognizes that all members of the patient system have an internal psychological life including, for example, the idea that the experience of important people in early development is internalized and colors later experience. Similarly, it provides a way to think about how patients maintain self-esteem. Constraints at this level may prevent members of the patient system from recognizing, experiencing, and integrating thoughts, feelings, and actions, which may also prevent them from taking the necessary steps to resolve constraints on other levels of the problem-maintenance space (Pinsof, 1995). Finally, the *spiritual* level of the problem-maintenance space involves whatever is held to be most important or sacred that fosters a sense of meaning, purpose, and significance in living. By including spirituality, we recognize that anorexia nervosa is deeply intertwined with the spiritual aspect of human experience.

Although research relevant to each level is integrated into a single metaframework in that level, in integrative problem-centered therapy there is no attempt to integrate information between levels of the problem-maintenance space (Pinsof, 2005). The clinical application of this model, including issues related to intervention sequencing, is discussed in the final chapter of this book, along with a detailed clinical case.

In the early meetings with the Goodstone family, after the beginnings of a therapeutic alliance have been established (see below), we discover an important constraint on the biological level of the problem-maintenance space that constraints the patient system from recovery. Because Jay was referred by his dentist, we know that malnutrition or purging is leading to the erosion of dental enamel. As I talk with Jay about his dental problems, I quickly note the obsessive and repetitive quality of his thinking. We discuss the importance of implementing behaviors, such as alkalinizing his mouth by gargling with baking soda in water, to reduce the harm of purging to his teeth. Throughout the conversation, Jay appears to become preoccupied with minute details. Noting his acute state of malnutrition, I hypothesize that Jay is unable to engage in (that is, constrained from) more productive problem solving by starvation, which exacerbates this quality of thinking. In addition, Jay is constrained from pursuing harm-reducing behavior by the obsessive and repetitive quality of his thinking.

Notably, Jay's obsessive and repetitive thinking may not be solely due to a constraint on the biological level of the problem-maintenance space, as patients with anorexia nervosa demonstrate broad set-shifting difficulties even after weight restoration (Green, Elliman, Wakeling, & Rogers, 1996).

As I talk with Jay individually in a later session, I learn that he is an avid participant in pro-anorexia Internet forums. Pro-anorexia forums comprise a movement, taking place largely in cyberspace, that adopts an at least partially positive attitude toward anorexia nervosa and other eating disorders, with content ranging from discussion forums, guidelines for beginning and maintaining anorexia, tips for rapid weight loss, dieting competitions, ways to avoid detection by family and friends, and motivational images (e.g., 'thinspiration') to inspire further weight loss (Strife & Rickard, 2011).

These forums, he tells me, provide him with a sense of connection and encouragement to continue in his weight loss practices. Although this is only the beginning of our exploration, we might hypothesize that this presents a constraint on the *culture and gender* level of the problem-maintenance space. Indeed, Jay's participation in pro-anorexia forums likely constrains his pursuit of healthy eating and weight behaviors. Later, Jay tells me about the teasing he has endured at school for being "soft" and his idealization of lean and muscular models. Here, we might suspect that Jay is constrained from developing healthier self-esteem by his history of being teased.

When I meet with Jay's father, Joseph, I begin to pick up on his subtle disapproval of psychological treatment. When I inquire further, Joseph admits that he's always felt that psychotherapy was for "women or those with too much time on their hands." Although further inquiry is called for, I hypothesize that we are encountering a constraint in the patient system on the *culture and gender* level of the problem-maintenance space. In particular, Joseph's beliefs about what is and is not masculine may, if they are not addressed, prevent his son from seeking the help that he so desperately needs. (See the next chapter for a longer discussion of the impact of problematic constructions of masculinity on therapeutic engagement and alliance building.)

At this early stage of treatment, we are able to construct a map of the problem-maintenance space as illustrated in Figure 2.3. The problem-maintenance space reflects our present understanding of the factors that prevent the patient system from resolving Jay's diagnosis of anorexia nervosa. As treatment unfolds, the problem-maintenance space will be expanded and revised as new constraints both come to light and are resolved within the patient system.

The Therapeutic Alliance

The therapeutic alliance is the holy grail of psychotherapy effectiveness because of its empirical support as well as its theoretical appeal to

Systemic
None identified

Biological
Jay is constrained from pursuing harm-reducing behaviors (e.g., dental hygiene measures) by the repetitive quality of his thinking. Jay's capacity for problem-solving conversations (i.e., without obsessive and repetitive features) is constrained by his physical state of starvation.

Culture and gender
Jay's participation in pro-anorexia forums constrains development of health eating and weight behaviors. Joseph's beliefs about masculinity constrain help-seeking behavior for his son.

Psychodynamic
Jay's history of teasing constrains development of healthy self-esteem.

Spiritual
None identified.

Figure 2.3 Goodstone family problem-maintenance space

practicing clinicians (Summers & Barber, 2010). In terms of its empirical support, research on the common factors in successful psychotherapy suggests that the therapeutic relationship is essential to treatment success (Sparks, Duncan, & Miller, 2008; Wollburg, Meyer, Osen, & Löwe, 2013). Indeed, the therapeutic alliance has been identified as one of the mechanisms that predicts outcome in all types of psychotherapy, correlating with improved treatment retention and outcome in individual psychotherapy (Martin, Garske, & Davis, 2000).

The therapeutic alliance in couple and family therapy is more complex than in individual psychotherapy, as clinicians are faced with building alliances with multiple family members who often have conflicting priorities and relational styles (Friedlander, Escudero, & Heatherington, 2006). Yet there is a rapidly expanding literature discussing the therapeutic alliance in couple and family therapy (e.g., Friedlander, Heatherington, Johnson, & Skowron, 1994; Hogue, Dauber, Stambaugh, Cecero, & Liddle, 2006).

What is the therapeutic alliance? The core component of the therapeutic alliance is collaboration. Through the vehicle of the therapeutic alliance, the patient and therapist collaborate to alleviate the patient's psychological distress and symptomatic behavior. The working alliance should provide a safe environment in which the therapeutic dyad can explore the content of the patient's concerns and also a relationship through which the patient's key relational templates can begin to emerge (Horvath & Greenberg, 1994). In addition, the therapeutic alliance develops as treatment proceeds; a positive alliance is not necessarily present at the beginning of therapy but, instead, may emerge as the dyad takes advantages of windows of opportunity. Ultimately, maintaining the alliance between the therapist and patient system takes priority over almost all interventions (Pinsof, 1995).

In my clinical practice, many patients present for their first session voicing extreme reservations about the desirability and possibility of successful treatment. At the level of content, I attempt to explore the concerns that give rise to these reservations, many of which are discussed below. By acknowledging and speaking to the patient's ambivalence, I seek to provide safety for the patient to speak to the complexity of his experience and also to establish the procedural aspect of the treatment situation (Hovath & Greenberg, 1994) – that is, all thoughts and feelings are welcomed. At the level of relational templates, on the other hand, as a mental health provider I may be experienced as many different figures in the patient's developmental history. In many cases, working through these relational templates is a task that unfolds throughout clinical work and provides a rich arena of exploration for understanding the patient's struggle with anorexia nervosa.

The therapeutic alliance has also been described as consisting of three components: goal, task, and bond (Bordin, 1979). From this point of view, the therapeutic alliance consists of a collaboratively established goal of treatment, a shared understanding of the tasks that each person is to perform, as well as an attachment bond.

This conception is particularly applicable to an integrative model. Throughout the process of treatment, the clinician hopes to establish an increasingly safe bond with each member of the patient system. Furthermore, the clinician seeks to develop an increasingly solidified goal among members of the patient system – the man or boy with anorexia nervosa but, also important, his family, friends, and other treatment providers – that the presenting problem will be resolved by addressing constraints on each level of the problem-maintenance space (Pinsof, 2005). In particular, the overarching goal of resolving the diagnosis of anorexia nervosa has at least three components: (1) fully normalized individualized weight which entails return to a biological "set point" after nutritional rehabilitation; (2) normal eating behavior and dietary content in a wide range of social situations; and (3) healthy thinking about food, weight, and shape, including a day-to-day life in which these concerns no longer dominate (Mehler & Andersen, 1999).

In service of this goal, the task shifts throughout the treatment process as the therapeutic team moves its focus between different levels of the problem-maintenance space. At one point in treatment, the task may require high levels of involvement from the parental system; at another, the patient himself may need to be deeply engaged in the process of nutritional rehabilitation. Although the task may change, it remains in service of the overarching goal and acknowledges the importance of maintaining a firm bond, if at all possible, with each member of the patient system.

Pinsof (1995) has described four factors that can be used to facilitate the progression of the bond component of the therapeutic alliance. First, the *relational focus* of therapy, which increases the focus on members of the patient systems' experience of the therapist, which tends to make the therapist more psychologically salient. Second, increasing the *frequency of sessions* tends to strengthen the bond component of the alliance. Third, *shifting the context of therapy* – in particular, decreasing the number of people in the direct patient system – often increases the bond between the therapist and members of the direct patient system. And finally, *time* is, naturally, a key component in the development of a bond between clinician and members of the patient system.

Whether the capacity to build strong therapeutic alliances can be taught is a complex question. There is some evidence that if the basic capacities are in place, clinicians can increasingly develop their skill in alliance building (Summers & Barber, 2010). Indeed, the foundational element of alliance building is interpersonal skill, which begins with social and emotional intelligence (Gardner, 1993; Goleman, 2006), including the ability to name and resonate with other's emotions, think about their motivations and conflicts, and respond with empathy and emotional understanding. Beyond this, alliance building requires a learned ability to balance closeness and separation, nurturance and reflection, ambition and acceptance throughout the psychotherapy process (Summers & Barber, 2010).

Because an integrative model is applied to an entire patient system, instead of only an identified patient, the therapeutic alliance is more complex than in individual psychotherapy. In his discussion of the therapeutic alliance, Pinsof (1995) has identified four interpersonal dimensions on which the therapeutic alliance is relevant: individual, subsystem, whole system, and within system. At each of these levels, the three components of goal, task, and bond are relevant. This is illustrated in Figure 2.4.

At the level of the *individual alliance*, the clinician must attempt to establish a therapeutic alliance with each individual member of the patient system. At the *subsystem* level, the clinician attempts to establish an alliance with the various subsystems – for example, the parental subsystem – in the patient system. In the *whole system* level, the clinician seeks an alliance with the entire patient system, which is more than the sum of the various individual and subsystem alliances. And finally, within system alliances point out the need to pay attention to alliances between the individuals and within the subsystems in the patient system as well as the alliances between treatment care providers.

As Pinsof (1995) points out, this conceptualization of the therapeutic alliance introduces the possibility of a *split alliance*, which refers to periods in treatment during which the clinician has a positive therapeutic alliance with one subsystem and a negative alliance with another subsystem within the same patient system. In some split alliances, treatment can still proceed

	Tasks	Goals	Bonds
Individual			
Subsystem			
Whole System			
Within System			

Figure 2.4 Components of the therapeutic alliance

Source: Pinsof (1995). Reprinted with permission.

successfully whereas in others it cannot. In addition, the alliance can be split in one or more of its three components of tasks, goals, and bonds.

Treatment Team

Evidence demonstrates better outcomes with an experienced multidisciplinary treatment team than with efforts by a single clinician (Mehler & Andersen, 1999; Halmi, 2009). Indeed, the contemporary emphasis on building multidisciplinary treatment teams to address severe psychiatric disorders is naturally aligned with an integrative approach. Because an integrative model recognizes that a multitude of factors – biological, familial, cultural, psychodynamic, and spiritual – are involved in anorexia nervosa, it is natural for the treatment team to consist of several members, each of whom has expertise in one or more of these areas. Treatment teams consist of psychiatrists, psychologists, social workers, occupational therapists, physicians or pediatricians, registered dieticians, as well as educators, clergy, even financial advisors to facilitate expensive inpatient treatment.

Psychologists, for example, ought to be informed about the biological complications involved in anorexia nervosa. Because of training and expertise, however, recognition and lifting of constraints in this area of the problem-maintenance space should be guided by a physician or, of equal importance, a registered dietician. Similarly, a registered dietician will often need the assistance of a physician to address acute medical complications. As another example, some patients claim to adhere to particular diets, such as vegetarianism, because of their religious beliefs. While the psychologist can explore the psychodynamic layers involved in the patient's religious belief, insofar as these may present constraints to problem resolution, a cleric may need to be involved in the direct patient system for a period of time to facilitate restoration of healthy eating.

Except in full-fledged treatment facilities, adding members to a treatment team takes significant time and effort. Typically, members of the treatment team are added one at a time, in what is known as a "stepped care" model. In this way of thinking, professionals are added to the treatment team, beginning with the lowest intensity intervention and progressing, as required, to more intensive forms of intervention until progress is made on resolving the patient's anorexia nervosa (Wilson, Vitousek, & Loeb, 2000).

Because it encompasses all human systems that are part of the maintenance or resolution of the presenting problem, the patient system includes all members of the multidisciplinary treatment team. In this way, the model presented in this chapter highlights the fact that the clinician must develop a therapeutic alliance (consisting of a goal, bond, and tasks) with all subsystems of the treatment team as well. Indeed, it is essential for members of the treatment team to share a broad treatment philosophy. In addition, a split alliance can occur between the clinician and subsystems of the treatment team; in most cases, these must be addressed for treatment to proceed successfully.

Returning to the Goodstone family, 14-year-old Jay arrives with his parents, Kit and Joseph. As we sit down to our first meeting, Jay seems withdrawn and disaffected. When I ask him what brought him and his family to therapy, he turns away and does not respond. Immediately I can see that substantial therapeutic work will need to take place for me to begin to develop the bond component of the individual alliance with Jay. To begin this process, I make a mental note to meet with Jay individually as soon as feasible.

Jay's mother, Kit, in contrast, is immediately engaged in the treatment process, rapidly cataloging her worries about her son. At one point, she tells me directly how much the family needs my help. Although her husband, Joseph, is reserved at first, when I meet with the parental subsystem without Jay present and begin to address his concerns, he begins to cry as he worries about his "failures as a father." At this point, I believe that I am beginning to form a bond with all three members of the Goodstone family.

Early on, however, the task component of the therapeutic alliance is split within the patient system. As I talk with Kit, I learn that the family doctor has recommended a non-interference policy for the parental subsystem. According to her, "Kids need space to work these things out." Because Jay is at a medically dangerous weight, however, we have decided to proceed with FBT for weight restoration. Although further inquiry is necessary, I hypothesize that there is a split in the alliance on the task component with the family doctor. This will need to be addressed by bringing the family doctor into the direct patient system for exploration and discussion.

In the following chapter, we consider the complexities of assessment and diagnosis of anorexia nervosa in men and boys. Interwoven with assessment and diagnosis is the ongoing process of therapeutic engagement and alliance building. A number of issues complicate therapeutic engagement and alliance, including the countertransference reactions often provoked by this patient population as well as the stigma and ambivalence that often surrounds the treatment situation. In addition, the implications of traditional constructions of masculinity on engagement and alliance building will be explored. For treatment to be successful, these difficulties must be addressed.

Note

1 Because of the limited theorizing and empirical research available about anorexia nervosa in males, we modified Pinsof's (1995) original formulation of the problem-maintenance space. In particular, the *Organizational* and *Transgenerational* levels of the problem-maintenance space were unified into a single level, *Systemic*. The *Object Relations* and *Self* levels were also unified into one level, *Psychodynamic*. In addition, the *Spiritual* level of the problem-maintenance space was added to conceptualize this domain of human activity.

References

Andersen, A. E., Bowers, W., & Evans, K. (1997). Inpatient treatment of anorexia nervosa. In D. M. Garner & P. E. Garfinkel (Eds.), *Handbook of treatment for eating disorders* (2nd ed., pp. 327–353). New York: Guilford Press.

Bateson, G. (1972). *Steps to an ecology of mind: Collected essays in anthropology, psychiatry, evolution, and epistemology*. San Francisco, CA: Chandler Pub. Co.

Berman, M. I., Boutelle, K. N., & Crow, S. J. (2009). A case series investigating acceptance and commitment therapy as a treatment for previously treated, unremitted patients with anorexia nervosa. *European Eating Disorders Review, 17*(6), 426–434.

Bordin, E. (1979). The generalizability of the psychoanalytic concept of the working alliance. *Psychotherapy: Theory, Research and Practice, 16*, 252–260.

Bosanac, P., Norman, T., Burrows, G., & Beumont, P. (2005). Serotonergic and dopaminergic systems in anorexia nervosa: A role for atypical antipsychotics? *Australia and New Zealand Journal of Psychiatry, 39*, 146–153.

Breunlin, D. C. (1999). Toward a theory of constraints. *Journal of Marriage and Family Therapy, 25*(3), 365–382.

Breunlin, D. C., Pinsof, W., Russell, W. P., & Lebow, J. (2011). Integrative problem-centered metaframeworks therapy I: Core concepts and hypothesizing. *Family Process, 50*(3), 293–313.

Breunlin, D. C., Schwartz, R. C., & Mac Kune-Karrer, B. M. (1997). *Metaframeworks: Transcending the models of family therapy (Revised and Updated)*. San Francisco, CA: Jossey-Bass.

Crisp, A. H. & Burns, T. (1990). Primary anorexia nervosa in the male and female: A comparison of clinical features and prognosis. In A. E. Andersen (Ed.), *Males with eating disorders* (pp. 77–99). New York: Brunner/Mazel.

Dally, P. & Gomez, J. (1979). *Anorexia nervosa*. New York: William Heinemann Medical Books.

Eisler, I. (1995). Family models of eating disorders. In G. Szmukler, C. Dare, & J. Treasure (Eds.), *Handbook of eating disorders: Theory, treatment, and research* (pp. 155–176). Chichester: John Wiley & Sons.

Eisler, I., Lock, J., & le Grange, D. (2010). Family based treatments for adolescents with anorexia nervosa: Single-family and multi-family approaches. In C. M. Grilo & J. E. Mitchell (Eds.), *The treatment of eating disorders: A clinical handbook* (pp. 150–174). New York: The Guilford Press.

Fairburn, C. G., Cooper, Z., Doll, H. A., O'Connor, M. E., Palmer, R. L., & Dalle Grave, R. (2013). Enhanced cognitive behaviour therapy for adults with anorexia nervosa: A UK–Italy study. *Behaviour Research and Therapy*, *51*(1), R2–R8.

Fishman, H. C. (2004). *Enduring change in eating disorders: Interventions with long-term results*. New York: Routledge.

Friedlander, M. L., Escudero, V., & Heatherington, L. (2006). *Therapeutic alliances in couple and family therapy: An empirically informed guide to practice*. Washington, DC: American Psychological Association.

Friedlander, M. L., Heatherington, L., Johnson, B., & Skowron, E. A. (1994). Sustaining engagement: A change event in family therapy. *Journal of Counseling Psychology*, *41*(4), 438–448.

Gardner, H. (1993). *Multiple intelligences: The theory in practice*. New York: Basic Books.

Garner, D. M. (1997). Psychoeducational principles in treatment. In D. M. Garner & P. E. Garfinkel (Eds.), *Handbook of treatment for eating disorders* (2nd ed.). New York: The Guilford Press.

Garner, D. M., Vitousek, K. M., & Pike, K. M. (1997). Cognitive-behavioral therapy for anorexia nervosa. In D. M. Garner & P. E. Garfinkel (Eds.), *Handbook of treatment for eating disorders* (2nd ed., pp. 145–177). New York: The Guilford Press.

Goleman, D. (2006). *Emotional intelligence*. New York: Bantam.

Green, M. W., Elliman, N. A., Wakeling, A., & Rogers, P. J. (1996). Cognitive functioning, weight change and therapy in anorexia nervosa. *Journal of Psychiatric Research*, *30*(5), 401–410.

Greenberg, S. T. & Schoen, E. G. (2008). Males and eating disorders: Gender-based therapy for eating disorder recovery. *Professional Psychology: Research and Practice*, *39*(4), 464–471.

Halmi, K. A. (2009). Anorexia nervosa: An increasing problem in children and adolescents. *Dialogues in Clinical Neuroscience*, *11*(1), 100–103.

Hayes, S. C., Strosahl, K. D., & Wilson, K. G. (2011). *Acceptance and commitment therapy: The process and practice of mindful change*. New York: Guilford Press.

Heffner, M., Sperry, J., Eifert, G. H., & Detweiler, M. (2002). Acceptance and commitment therapy in the treatment of an adolescent female with anorexia nervosa: A case example. *Cognitive and Behavioral Practice*, *9*(3), 232–236.

Hoffman, I. Z. (2009). Doublethinking our way to "scientific" legitimacy: The dessication of human experience. *Journal of the American Psychoanalytic Association, 57*, 1043–1069.

Hogue, A., Dauber, S., Stambaugh, L. F., Cecero, J. J., & Liddle, H. A. (2006). Early therapeutic alliance and treatment outcome in individual and family therapy for adolescent behavior problems. *Journal of Consulting and Clinical Psychology*, *74*(1), 121–129.

Horvath, A. O. & Greenberg, L. S. (1994). *The working alliance: Theory, research, and practice* (Vol. 173). New York: John Wiley & Sons.

Kaplan, A. S. & Howlett, A. (2010). Pharmacotherapy for anorexia nervosa. In C. M. Grilo & J. E. Mitchell (Eds.), *The treatment of eating disorders: A clinical handbook* (pp. 175–186). New York: The Guilford Press.

Kaplan, A. S. & Olmsted, M. P. (1997). Partial hospitalization. In C. M. Grilo & J. E. Mitchell (Eds.), *The treatment of eating disorders: A clinical handbook* (pp. 354–360). New York: The Guilford Press.

Leit, R. A., Gray, J. J., & Pope, H. G. (2002). The media's representation of the ideal male body: A cause for muscle dysmorphia? *International Journal of Eating Disorders, 31*(3), 334–338.

Linehan, M. (1993). *Cognitive-behavioral treatment of borderline personality disorder*. New York: Guilford Press.

Martin, D. J., Garske, J. P., & Davis, M. K. (2000). Relation of the therapeutic alliance with outcome and other variables: A meta-analytic review. *Journal of Consulting and Clinical Psychology, 68*(3), 438–450.

McIntosh, V. V. W., Jordan, J., & Bulik, C. M. (2010). Specialist supportive clinical management for anorexia nervosa. In C. M. Grilo & J. E. Mitchell (Eds.), *The treatment of eating disorders: A clinical handbook* (pp. 150–174). New York: The Guilford Press.

Mehler, P. S. & Andersen, A. E. (1999). *Eating disorders: A guide to medical care and complications*. Baltimore, MD: JHU Press.

Nathan, P. E. & Gorman, J. M. (2002). *A guide to treatments that work* (2nd ed.). London: Oxford University Press.

Olmsted, M. P., McFarlane, T. L., Carter, J. C., Trottier, K., Woodside, D. B., & Dimitropoulos, G. (2010). Inpatient and day hospital treatment for anorexia nervosa. In C. M. Grilo & J. E. Mitchell (Eds.), *The treatment of eating disorders: A clinical handbook* (pp. 198–211). New York: The Guilford Press.

Pike, K. M., Carter, J. C., & Olmsted, M. P. (2010). Cognitive-behavioral therapy for anorexia nervosa. In C. M. Grilo & J. E. Mitchell (Eds.), *The treatment of eating disorders: A clinical handbook* (pp. 83–107). New York: The Guilford Press.

Pinsof, W. M. (1995). *Integrative problem-centered therapy: A synthesis of family, individual, and biological therapies*. New York: Basic Books.

Pinsof, W. M. (2005). Integrative problem-centered therapy. In J. C. Norcross & M. R. Goldfield (Eds.), *Handbook of psychotherapy integration* (pp. 282–402). Oxford: Oxford University Press.

Pope, H. G. & Katz, D. L. (1994). Psychiatric and medical effects of anabolic-androgenic steroid use: A controlled study of 160 athletes. *Archives of General Psychiatry, 51*(5), 375–382.

Räisänen, U. & Hunt, K. (2014). The role of gendered constructions of eating disorders in delayed help-seeking in men: A qualitative interview study. *British Medical Journal Open, 4*(4) e004342, doi: 10.1136/bmjopen-2013-004342.

Rock, C. L. (2010). Nutritional rehabilitation for anorexia nervosa. In C. M. Grilo & J. E. Mitchell (Eds.), *The treatment of eating disorders: A clinical handbook* (pp. 187–197). New York: The Guilford Press.

Rossi, G., Balottin, U., Rossi, M., Chiappedi, M., Fazzi, E., & Lanzi, G. (2007). Pharmacological treatment of anorexia nervosa: A retrospective study in preadolescents and adolescents. *Clinical Pediatrics, 46*(9), 806–11.

Salbach, H., Klinkowski, N., Pfeiffer, E., Lehmkuhl, U., & Korte, A. (2007). Body image and attitudinal aspects of eating disorders in rhythmic gymnasts. *Psychopathology, 40*(6), 388–393.

Sparks, J. A., Duncan, B. L., & Miller, S. D. (2008). Common factors in psychotherapy. In J. L. Lebow (Ed.), *Twenty-first century psychotherapies: Contemporary approaches to theory and practice* (pp. 453–497). New York: John Wiley & Sons.

Strife, R. S. & Rickard, K. (2011). The conceptualization of anorexia: The pro-ana perspective. *Journal of Women and Social Work, 26*(2), 213–217.

Summers, R. F. & Barber, J. P. (2010). *Psychodynamic therapy: A guide to evidence-based practice.* New York: The Guilford Press.

Tchanturia, K. & Hambrook, D. (2010). Cognitive remediation therapy for anorexia nervosa. In C. M. Grilo & J. E. Mitchell (Eds.), *The treatment of eating disorders: A clinical handbook* (pp. 130–150). New York: The Guilford Press.

Wilson, G. T., Vitousek, K. M., & Loeb, K. L. (2000). Stepped care treatment for eating disorders. *Journal of Consulting and Clinical Psychology, 68*(4), 564–572.

Wisniewski, L. & Kelly, E. (2003). The application of dialectical behavior therapy to the treatment of eating disorders. *Cognitive and Behavioral Practice, 10*(2), 131–138.

Wollburg, E., Meyer, B., Osen, B., & Löwe, B. (2013). Psychological change mechanisms in anorexia nervosa treatments: How much do we know? *Journal of Clinical Psychology, 69*(7), 762–773.

Wooldridge, T. (2014). The enigma of ana: A psychoanalytic exploration of pro-ana forums. *The Journal of Infant, Child, and Adolescent Psychotherapy, 13*(3), 202–216.

Wooldridge, T. & Lytle, P. (2012). An overview of anorexia nervosa in males. *Eating Disorders: Journal of Treatment & Prevention, 20*(5), 368–378.

Zerbe, K. J. (2010). Psychodynamic therapy for eating disorders. In C. M. Grilo & J. E. Mitchell (Eds.), *The treatment of eating disorders: A clinical handbook* (pp. 339–358). New York: The Guilford Press.

3 Diagnosis, Engagement, and Alliance

In this chapter, we consider the nuances of assessment and diagnosis that arise with men and boys who exhibit disturbances in eating, weight, and shape, including the rapidly evolving diagnostic definitions of eating disorders in the DSM-5. We consider the recent changes that have taken place in the diagnostic criteria for anorexia nervosa. Throughout the discussion, we emphasize the issues that arise in the process of assessment and diagnosis for men and boys in particular.

Before treatment can commence, men and boys with anorexia nervosa (and in many cases, their families) must first make contact with a treatment provider. Once initial contact has been made, therapist and patient confront the difficult task of establishing a preliminary working alliance. With this in mind, in the remainder of the chapter we turn to the complexities faced by males with anorexia nervosa in reaching out to treatment providers and, once initial contact has been made, in developing a working alliance.

Assessment and Diagnosis

As Darcy and Lin (2013) point out, assessment of eating disorders in males raises the question of what is an eating disorder and what is not. And as the recent revision of the *Diagnostic and Statistical Manual of Mental Disorders* from the fourth to fifth edition demonstrates, the diagnostic definitions of eating disorders are rapidly evolving. In fact, the DSM-5 (American Psychiatric Association, 2013) appears to capture a larger number of males in specific diagnoses, instead of through the Eating Disorder Not Otherwise Specified category in the DSM-IV.

For example, in the DSM-5 a new diagnosis, *binge eating disorder (BED)*, was included. According to the DSM-5, binge eating disorder involves recurrent episodes of binge eating, or episodes of rapid food intake in large amounts not in response to hunger. These episodes are often followed by embarrassment and shame about the amount of food consumed as well as feelings of guilt, depression, and disgust with one's behavior. In addition to causing considerable distress, compensatory behaviors, such as purging and laxative abuse, are not present. According to epidemiological research, men and boys constitute a substantial portion of the clinical population for binge eating disorder (Raevuori, Keski-Rahkonen, & Hoek, 2014). In fact, the disorder may affect up to 2 percent of the male population, which makes it more than 2.5 times more common than other eating disorders in males combined (Swanson, Crow, le Grange, Swendsen, & Merikangas, 2011).

In the DSM-5, *bulimia nervosa* is characterized by frequent episodes of binge eating followed by compensatory behaviors such as self-induced vomiting, laxative abuse, excessive exercise, fasting as well as other methods in an attempt to avoid weight gain. While the DSM-IV required patients to exhibit binge eating episodes and their compensatory behaviors twice weekly, according to the DSM-5, patients who exhibit these behaviors once weekly meet the criteria for diagnosis. Bulimia nervosa affects approximately 0.2 percent of adolescent boys and young men, and males account for 10–15 percent of all patients with the disorder (Carlat & Camargo, 1991).

In addition, in the DSM-5 *muscle dysmorphia* (Pope, Katz, & Hudson, 1993), a pathological preoccupation with muscle development that manifests primarily in males, is included as a specifier for body dysmorphic disorder. Finally, the DSM-5 also includes the category of *other specified feeding or eating disorder (OSFED)*, which captures atypical anorexia nervosa, in which all diagnostic criteria are met except for underweight, as well as night eating syndrome, which is constituted by a substantial male population (Tholin et al., 2009; Runfola, Allison, Hardy, Lock, & Peebles, 2014).

Several revisions have taken place in the diagnostic criteria for anorexia nervosa in the DSM-5. In the DSM-IV, for example, amenorrhea was included in the diagnostic criteria for women and girls with anorexia nervosa. Similarly, the diagnosis included a stringent weight requirement, which excluded many male patients from diagnosis. The DSM-5, in contrast, removed both of these from its list of criteria for anorexia nervosa. The DSM-V (American Psychiatric Association, 2013) criteria for anorexia nervosa include:

> Persistent restriction of energy intake leading to significantly low body weight (in context of what is minimally expected for age, sex, developmental trajectory, and physical health).
>
> Either an intense fear of gaining weight or of becoming fat, or persistent behaviour that interferes with weight gain (even though significantly low weight).
>
> Disturbance in the way one's body weight or shape is experienced, undue influence of body shape and weight on self-evaluation, or persistent lack of recognition of the seriousness of the current low body weight.

In addition, the DSM-5 includes subtype specifications for individuals who do not regularly engage in binge eating or purging behaviors (the restricting subtype) as well as for patients who do engage in these behaviors (the binge–purge subtype).

A number of conditions are comorbid with anorexia nervosa. In fact, anorexia is typically accompanied by, on average, two additional psychiatric diagnoses (Margolis, Spencer, Depaulo, Simpson, & Andersen, 1994). Among these, mood and anxiety disorders are particularly prevalent. In part, these conditions may be exacerbated by severe malnutrition (Keys, Brozek, Henschel, Mickelson, & Taylor, 1950). In addition, social phobia is often considered in the assessment process, as some patients report a fear of eating in public, fearing social disapproval of their restrictive or binge eating or that others will experience disgust in watching them engage in the process of eating (Keel & McCormick, 2010). In addition, research suggests that a significant number of male patients with eating disorders engage in non-suicidal self-injury (Claes et al., 2012). Ultimately, starvation changes the personality drastically, which must be accounted for in the diagnostic process (Andersen & Mickalide, 1983). A number of symptoms, such as counting calories, are better conceptualized as an aspect of anorexia nervosa than as warranting a separate diagnosis (Keel & McCormick, 2010).

Ultimately, the process of diagnosis requires a working knowledge of the diagnostic manual as well the skills and knowledge to perform a competent initial assessment. Although the assessment process is a complicated one that has been described in considerable detail elsewhere (e.g., Crowther & Sherwood, 1997; Mitchell & Peterson, 2007; Keel & McCormick, 2010), in this volume we provide an overview of the process with an emphasis on issues in the assessment process that are particular to men and boys.

Differing approaches may be employed during the assessment process, ranging from an unstructured interview to a structured diagnostic interview. At present, the most commonly used formal measures of eating disorder symptomatology appear to be less applicable to males. For example, males consistently score lower than females even when their levels of psychopathology are equivalent. In addition, the measures appear to be less internally reliable among males (Darcy & Lin, 2013). With these concerns in mind, a number of assessments are currently being adapted and validated for male populations (see Darcy & Lin, 2013 for an overview of the application of formal assessment protocols to men and boys with eating disorders).

Regardless of the approach employed, the assessment process should gather information about a number of factors. First, the clinician should obtain demographic features, treatment history, and the circumstances that led to initial contact with a treatment provider. In addition, information about current body weight and weight history should be obtained. This includes highest and lowest weight, highest stable weight prior to onset of the disorder, and a chronology of weight changes (Crowther & Sherwood, 1997).

A thick description of eating and weight-control behaviors should be gathered. Indeed, a brief picture of the issues that surround eating behavior can be gathered by asking the patient to comprehensively describe a usual day's food intake (Nicholson, 2013). Because of the possibility that the patient may intentionally or unintentionally distort this information, it should also be gathered, when possible, from family members. In addition, clinicians should enquire about patient's self-imposed dietary rules that may contribute to caloric restriction, including distinctions between "good" and "bad" foods (Crowther & Sherwood, 1997).

With regard to weight control, information about dieting, vomiting, spitting food, exercise, and substances used to control weight such as laxatives, diuretics, drugs, and alcohol should be obtained (Garner, Vitousek, & Pike, 1997). Because males tend to exhibit different motivations for bodily change, and because of the close relationship between anorexia nervosa and muscle dysmorphia (Murray et al., 2012), it is essential to assess for the use of anabolic steroids, especially in athletic populations. Also critical is assessing use of appearance and performance enhancing drugs (Hildebrandt et al., 2011).

Finally, the interviewer should assess attitudes toward body weight and shape. Indeed, distortions in body image have been shown to have an impact on the etiology, maintenance, and prognosis of eating disorders (Stice, 2002). In addition to assessing for overvaluation of the significance of weight and shape, clinicians should note the level of disparagement of the body, including its various parts, misperceptions of body shape, frequency of weighing and intrusive thoughts about weight, and perception of others' attitudes about the patient's weight (Crowther & Sherwood, 1997).

Many boys with anorexia nervosa who present for treatment are at a developmental stage in which they are negotiating individuation from the parental system (Fairburn & Gowers, 2008). With this in mind, it is essential that the mental health provider approach the task of assessment with tact, acknowledging the validity of the patient's perspective. Indeed, time should be set aside to meet with the patient individually and to fully validate his experience of anorexia nervosa – an occurrence which, in all likelihood, has not yet happened. This not only facilitates the development of a working alliance with the patient itself but also provides an opportunity for the patient to discuss the ego-syntonic nature of the disorder, which is often distressing to those in a caretaking role. Of course, it is equally important that the clinician must recognize the role of the parents in providing developmental history, a valuable perspective, and an invaluable component of treatment.

In the process of assessment and diagnosis, clinicians must remember that men and boys may seek to change their bodies for different reasons than women and girls. For example, males often deny the fear of becoming fat (Darcy & Lin 2013); in contrast, they more easily acknowledge a desire to become increasingly fit, healthy, and to gain strength. In seeking these goals, they often become entrenched in a disordered pattern of eating and exercise (Darcy & Lin, 2013). For example, males may be more likely to engage in compulsive forms of exercise without adequate caloric compensation. In addition, while women and girls almost always express a desire for thinness and tend to focus on particular body parts such as the waist and thighs, men and boys, in contrast, often describe wanting increased lean muscle, with an emphasis on chest, biceps, and abdominal muscles (Parkinson, Tovée, & Cohen-Tovée, 1998).

Engagement and Alliance

The majority of individuals who meet the criteria for a mental health disorder do not seek treatment (Bland, Newman, & Orn, 1997). Although the population of males with anorexia nervosa who fail to seek treatment is difficult to estimate, it is likely at least as large as with other mental health disorders. Indeed, research shows that males are more likely to seek treatment at a later age than their female counterparts (Gueguen et al., 2012). Similarly, prematurely terminated treatment is a pervasive feature of both inpatient and outpatient treatment programs for anorexia nervosa (Sly, 2009). In fact, dropout rates as high as 50–58 percent have been cited in the literature for female patients (Button, Marshall, Shinkwin, Black, & Palmer, 1997; Sly, Morgan, Mountford, & Lacey, 2013).

The importance of a strong working alliance in successful treatment of anorexia nervosa is clear (Elvins & Green, 2008; Antoniou & Cooper, 2013). In adolescents taking part in FBT, alliance was related to early weight gain as well as final outcome (Pereira, Lock, & Oggins, 2006). Similar results have been reported elsewhere (Sly, Morgan, Mountford & Lacey 2013; Forsberg, et al., 2014). And in the literature on common factors – factors unrelated to the specific intervention applied but nonetheless essential to its success – the therapeutic relationship and instilling hope are identified as key to positive outcome (Sparks, Duncan, & Miller, 2008; Wollburg, Meyer, Osen, & Löwe, 2013).

In spite of the clear importance of the therapeutic relationship, many therapists hold negative attitudes toward clients with eating disorders, often viewing them as difficult and defiant, frustrating, and reluctant to engage in treatment (Fairburn & Harrison, 2003). After all, anorexia nervosa is ego-syntonic in nature, in contrast to most psychiatric disorders, which are experienced as intrusive and undesirable by the patient. As a result, an entrenched and polarized battle often develops between patients and health care providers (Tierney, 2008). In addition, the high risk nature of anorexia nervosa, with mortality rates that exceed other psychiatric disorders (Smink, van Hoeken, & Hoek, 2012), creates intense anxiety for those in caretaking positions. In response to this anxiety, clinicians may focus on weight as the primary indicator of the patient's illness (Darcy et al., 2010), with weight restoration as the sole goal of treatment.

This approach neglects the subjective experience of the patient. Indeed, the working alliance is strengthened through factors such as warmth, empathy, respect, curiosity, acceptance, and supportiveness (Lask & Hage, 2013). With a single-minded emphasis on symptom reduction and weight restoration, however, it is difficult to attend adequately to issues related to treatment engagement and developing the therapeutic alliance.

In the following pages, we discuss three factors that interfere with both treatment engagement and the development of a working alliance with mental health providers for men and boys with anorexia nervosa: the ambivalence inherent in the experience of anorexia nervosa, the stigma and shame of having a psychiatric disorder, and one that has been culturally labeled as a "woman's problem" in particular, and the adversarial relationship between traditional constructions of masculinity and help-seeking behavior.

Ambivalence

The experience of anorexia nervosa is fraught with ambivalence (Williams & Reid, 2010). Ambivalence is defined as having both positive and negative feelings, or conflicting motivations, about something. In contrast to most mental health problems, anorexia is seen as positive, at least in part, by patients (Garner & Bemis, 1982). Several studies have documented the ambivalence experienced by individuals with anorexia nervosa (Colton & Pistrang, 2004; Reid, Burr, Williams, & Hammersley, 2008). In many cases, patients report feeling uncertain about whether anorexia is a "friend" or an "enemy" and whether it is a problem that needs treatment (Colton & Pistrang, 2004), often spending a great deal of time weighing its advantages and disadvantages (Cockell, Geller, & Linden, 2003). At times, patients may experience the disorder as an empowering mark of distinction that is to be further cultivated (Warin, 2004).

The transtheoretical model of change illuminates how people change both on their own and with the help of psychological intervention (Prochaska, 1999). According to this model, people change by progressing through a series of stages. Each stage represents a period of time during the change process as well as a set of tasks to be accomplished before moving to the next stage.

In this model, five stages of change are described: precontemplation, contemplation, preparation, action, and maintenance. In the *precontemplation* stage, an individual is not prepared to change. In this stage, most people have little awareness of the extent of their problems, though friends and family are often concerned and may even broach their concerns with the prospective patient. In the *contemplation* stage, an individual is seriously thinking about beginning the change process, but a commitment to action, whether intrapsychic or as evidenced by seeking out treatment, has not yet taken place. In the *preparation* stage, an individual develops the intention to take action toward change and may even be reporting small behavior changes. In the *action* stage, an individual is actively engaging in change-related behaviors but the desired outcome has not yet been fully actualized. Finally, in the *maintenance* stage, an individual is working to maintain positive outcomes and prevent relapse (Norcross, Krebs, & Prochaska, 2011).

Typically, friends, family and the medical community avoid grappling with the ambivalence inherent in anorexia nervosa by focusing exclusively on weight restoration. In this defensive mode, weight is used as the primary indicator of a patient's degree of illness and becomes the primary focus of treatment (Darcy et al., 2010). Indeed, well-intentioned comments from friends and family often focus on weight, ignoring the social and emotional dimensions of the disorder (Rich, 2006).

In spite of this, the identification and exploration of ambivalence is a powerful means of engaging individuals with anorexia nervosa in treatment programs (Pike, Loeb, & Vitousek, 1996; Treasure & Ward, 1997). Most men and boys who make contact with a treatment provider for the first time are in the precontemplation or contemplation stages of change. In the precontemplation stage, patients are (1) not aware that their behaviors are problematic; (2) defensive or in denial about the extent of their problems; and (3) demoralized about their ability to change (Prochaska, 1999). In this stage, we often encounter men and boys who meet the diagnostic criteria for anorexia nervosa but, because the disorder is popularly thought of as afflicting women and girls, are unaware that they suffer from a psychiatric disorder!

In the early stages of engagement and alliance building, then, providers must gently name the patient's behaviors and begin to educate patients about the consequences of their behaviors while acknowledging denial and defensiveness. Treatment providers who are willing to engage in "taboo talk" – in other words, straightforwardly acknowledging the part of the patient that wants to continue engaging in symptomatic behaviors – were more likely to form strong and effective therapeutic alliances (Sly et al., 2014). In addition, providers must hold realistic hope for the patient's potential for change and evolution (Sparks, Duncan, & Miller, 2008).

In the contemplation stage, patients are intending to change their behaviors in the future. As a group, patients in this stage evaluate the benefits of their behaviors as about equal to the risks. Although they admit that their behavior can be destructive, they nonetheless remain highly ambivalent (Prochaska, 1999). To facilitate movement to the preparation stage, clinicians must begin to help these individuals to further acknowledge the risks and drawbacks associated with their behaviors, without denying their perceived benefits. Indeed, clinicians must acknowledge that while anorexia nervosa may provide a degree of control and power, it also wreaks havoc on health, relationships, and life satisfaction. In other words, the benefits and risks of anorexia nervosa must be openly acknowledged and benefits and risks must be weighed – and this must be done, if the patient's medical condition allows it, without premature resolution.

In the early stages of treatment, Ted, a 22-year-old graduate student who called me at the insistence of his physician, and I discuss his ambivalence about change. Although he began treatment in the precontemplative stage, after a few sessions he increasingly expresses a more ambivalent attitude toward his illness.

THERAPIST: From what you've told me, I can tell that you feel really good after you've exercised and, as you say, eaten well. It feels empowering to be in control of your body and on top of your exercise routine. Sometimes, as you said, it's worth it to feel hungry and tired all the time.

TED: Yeah. I think that's right. But it also limits me, you know? I mean, I don't have time to spend with friends because I'm at the track running every evening. And I'm too tired to do much of anything at the end of the day…

THERAPIST: As you're saying, it does have some drawbacks – serious ones.

TED: Right, it does. I am thinking about giving it up, but I'm not sure that I ever really could. I think that would be really hard for me.

In this excerpt, by gently acknowledging the perceived benefits of his illness, I attempt to provide Ted with room to give voice to other, conflicting perspectives he may hold inside himself. As we can see, he begins to contemplate the possibility of change and, over time, may move on to the preparation stage.

Stigma

The experience of stigma is central to the experience of anorexia nervosa in men and boys. Indeed, men with anorexia nervosa face the additional stigma of suffering from an illness primarily associated with women. Stigma is deeply related to the experience of shame (Scheff, 2014) and stigma and shame are consistently identified as obstacles to treatment engagement (Satcher, 1999; Jennings et al., 2015). In fact, research shows that an important reason many men and boys do not seek treatment for anorexia nervosa is stigma (Räisänen & Hunt, 2014). While seeking treatment for mental illness carries its own stigma in our society, men with anorexia nervosa face the additional stigma of seeking help for a "woman's problem" (Andersen, Cohn, & Holbrook, 2000).

In all likelihood, stigma also obscures the recognition of the condition in friends, family, and treatment providers. When a problem is recognized, the social consequences associated with treatment are considered; if high stigma is perceived, the likelihood of denial or self-reliance may well increase (Jennings et al., 2015).

For these reasons, stigma must be addressed early in treatment. At this point, stigma should be named and the layers of shame and embarrassment beneath acknowledged. An important aspect of addressing stigma is education. Indeed, men and boys with anorexia nervosa often lack a narrative that accurately represents their experience, especially in a world that provides little attention to the experience of men with the disorder.

Ted, the 22-year-old graduate student mentioned above, and I have had a difficult first session. As our time draws to a close, Ted falls into another protracted silence. I ask, "I wonder how you feel about everything that's happened in the past week – your doctor sending you to me, hearing that you've got an eating disorder from both of us. It brings up a lot, doesn't it?" When Ted responds dismissively, I persist:

THERAPIST: For a lot of guys, it's an embarrassing experience to come to a therapist for the first time – to talk about these things with someone you don't know yet. It's easier to imagine handling it on your own. But we can also see that self-reliance hasn't worked; it almost never does with problems like this.

TED: What if people find out that I'm coming here?

THERAPIST: What if they do?

TED: Well, that would be completely humiliating.

THERAPIST: Right. This eating disorder is a secret that you've been keeping for a long time. And although it's done a lot of damage to your health and your relationships, it's also helped you get through some difficult times.

TED: And both you and the doctor are telling me I have anorexia. Honestly, I didn't really know that. I thought about it, but I also thought that doesn't really happen to guys.

THERAPIST: Right. And that is a popular misconception. In fact, we think that as many as 25 percent of people who have anorexia nervosa are male.

In this excerpt, I attempt to first address aspects of the stigma and shame that accompany Ted's evolving self-understanding and contact with a treatment provider. In addition, I also attempt to acknowledge Ted's ambivalence about change, recognizing that while anorexia nervosa has been disastrous for his physical and psychological health, he has experienced the disorder as an invaluable coping mechanism for many years. And in the final exchange, I begin the process of psychoeducation about the disorder in males.

Traditional Constructions of Masculinity

There is a growing body of research that suggests that men are less likely to seek help from mental health professionals (Galdas, Cheater, & Marshall, 2005). In particular, men appear to hold more negative attitudes toward psychotherapy and mental health treatment in general than their female counterparts (Andrews, Issakidis, & Carter, 2001). In fact, research suggests that adherence to traditional constructions of masculinity and beliefs regarding masculinity are significant variables influencing the help-seeking behavior of men. Traditional masculinity is associated with less positive attitudes toward psychological help-seeking (Berger, Wagner, & Baker, 2005) and lower willingness to seek mental health treatment (Robertson & Fitzgerald, 1992). From this point of view, the construction of traditional masculinity and the effort to conform to socially prescribed gender roles prevents the expression of vulnerability and need for help (Galdas, Cheater, & Marshall, 2005). These factors, among others, likely contribute to the difficulties men and boys with anorexia nervosa may have as they engage and persist in treatment.

How can treatment providers address the impact of traditional constructions of masculinity on treatment engagement and on the formation of a working alliance? In the following pages, I will suggest that therapeutic interventions can target normative beliefs, which are deeply related to the male experience of stigma and, thus, help-seeking behavior (Hammer, Vogel, & Heimerdinger-Edwards, 2013).

Normativeness refers to the degree to which others are seen as sharing an experience or engaging in a set of behaviors (Cialdini & Trost, 1999). In this sense, normativeness can be thought of as inversely proportional to stigma and, therefore, the degree of normativeness with which an individual perceives help-seeking behavior increases the likelihood that an individual will pursue help (Nadler, 1990).

According to Mahalik (2000), there are three types of normative messages about masculinity. First, descriptive masculine norms are at work when a male observes what other males are doing in a particular situation. As a treatment provider, I often make reference to stories about other men and boys who have made the decision to speak with their friends and family about their struggles and to seek treatment. In this way, during the early stages of building the working alliance, descriptive masculine norms can be countered through concrete examples of men behaving differently.

Secondly, injunctive norms provide the cultural "shoulds" and "should nots" of masculinity. For example, men often experience the injunctive norm that they should be strong and independent (David & Brannon, 1976). Although it is possible to directly confront and argue against injunctive norms, research suggests that mental health interventions designed to decrease men's conformity to traditional constructions of masculinity do not significantly improve men's help-seeking behaviors (Smith et al., 2011). As a result, it is likely to be more effective to reframe help-seeking behavior so that it is consistent with injunctive norms. For example, treatment providers may describe treatment engagement as requiring strength and courage, which is consistent with traditional constructions of masculinity (Good & Wood, 1995). Similarly, a male who conforms to the notion of masculinity as stoicism may experience seeking treatment as representing a tremendous threat to his self-esteem. This scenario might be reframed as a choice between taking control of anorexia nervosa or submitting to its demands.

Thirdly, cohesive masculine norms influence perceptions of normativeness when men observe popular and well-respected men. This form of normativeness and its likely impact on treatment engagement highlights the importance of working culturally to overcome stigma and to provide examples of men with eating disorders who have sought treatment and led productive, satisfying lives. In fact, this appears to be increasingly happening in the popular media and through advocacy organizations.

In the following excerpt, Ted and I discuss his concerns about beginning treatment and, perhaps, opening up discussion with his fiancée about his struggles.

TED: You know, I'm not sure that I need to be here, really. I could take this up on my own, work on this problem. It's not that big of a deal... I mean, this is for people who really have emotional problems.

THERAPIST: Yeah, it's hard to imagine needing help from someone else with this problem. From the little we've talked about so far, I get the sense that you're used to tackling problems on your own... being self-sufficient and not complaining to other people has been the way you've handled things.

TED: Right. My fiancée says that I'm really stoic. And it's true I guess.

THERAPIST: I also get the sense that you've got a lot of courage, to have made it through all the things that you've been confronted with... And it takes a lot of courage to push back against that part of yourself that wants to do things on your own, to rely only on yourself.

Ultimately, traditional constructions of masculinity overtly work against treatment engagement. While this points to the need for working against stigma at a societal level, clinicians must also understand the components that comprise the traditional construction of masculinity and sensitively assess the patient's own allegiances. In this way, it is possible for clinicians to leverage the patient's strengths toward treatment engagement.

The Theory of Constraints

The model presented in this book rests on the theory of constraints (Breunlin, 1999). With an emphasis on negative explanation, the clinician's goal is to ask what prevents (that is, constrains) the patient system from resolving the identified patient's struggle with anorexia nervosa. Once a definitive diagnosis has been established, the clinician's task is to collaborate with the patient system to identify and lift those constraints.

Breunlin (1999) describes a four-step process for identifying constraints. First, as the clinician and members of the patient system discuss the problem, their task is to clearly define the problem and to elicit episodes in which problem resolution is attempted. As Pinsof (1995) has pointed out, the problem-maintaining behavior implies alternatives that would assist in problem resolution. Second, the clinician asks a question of the form, "What keeps you from...?" or "What would happen if...?" Third, the clinician and members of the patient system collaboratively identify the constraints that emerge from answers to these questions. The fourth step, finally, is to discuss together how the constraint might be lifted. As constraints are lifted, new constraints emerge and the process continues, recursively identifying and lifting constraints to problem resolution.

In the following excerpt, Ted and I engage in this four-step process in an effort to understand his "inability" to talk with his fiancée about his struggle with anorexia nervosa.

TED: I don't really have any support. I haven't told anyone. People say to me, "Wow, you've lost so much weight man..." But I just say that I've been studying a lot – no time for eating. I think my fiancée knows something's wrong and she's dropped hints, but I don't tell her.

THERAPIST: What keeps you from telling her?

TED: I thought you'd ask that. It would be humiliating. I mean, come on – she wants me to be a man. And I'm going to confess to her that I've got some kind of emotional problem? She'd run in the other direction.

THERAPIST: What keeps you from telling your fiancée, at least in part, is this idea that it would be humiliating because it's not "manly" to have an emotional problem, as you call it...

TED: I don't really see how that's going to change, doctor.

THERAPIST: Yes, you'd have to feel like you could talk to her about this without sacrificing your masculinity to move in that direction.

In this excerpt, Ted begins by describing feeling unsupported and, in particular, mentions that he has yet to tell his fiancée about his struggles. At this point, we might define the problem as "Ted feels unsupported and can't reach out to anyone, even his fiancée." In the second step, I ask, "What keeps you from telling her?" From Ted's response, we are able to hypothesize that his beliefs about masculinity and fear of shame constrain him from seeking his fiancée's support. In the fourth step, we state directly what must happen next for this constraint to lift – that is, Ted would have to feel that talking with his fiancée didn't risk humiliation and his masculinity.

During this process, our conversation has pointed to the existence of another constraint to which this process must be recursively applied. In particular, Ted has suggested that he can't imagine feeling like a man while also having an emotional problem. Indeed, we must now turn to what constrains Ted from maintaining his masculine identity while also having emotional struggles.

In the following chapter, we develop a metaframework that integrates the various theories of systemic functioning and family therapy with an eye toward anorexia nervosa in men and boys. We discuss the long history of family therapy with anorexia nervosa, including early approaches such as structural family therapy, the Milan approach, the feminist critique of family therapy, and the well-recognized and empirically supported Maudsley approach to family-based treatment. Finally, we review the empirical research on families of male patients with anorexia nervosa.

References

American Psychiatric Association (2013). *Diagnostic and statistical manual of mental disorders*, (5th ed.). Washington, DC: Author.

Andersen, A. E. & Mickalide, A. D. (1983). Anorexia nervosa in the male: An underdiagnosed disorder. *Psychosomatics*, 24, 1066–1075.

Andersen, A. E., Cohn, L., & Holbrook, T. (2000). *Making weight: Healing men's conflicts with food, weight, and shape*. Carlsbad, CA: Gürze Books.

Andrews, G., Issakidis, C., & Carter, G. (2001). Shortfall in mental health service utilisation. *The British Journal of Psychiatry*, 179(5), 417–425.

Antoniou, P. & Cooper, M. (2013). Psychological treatments for eating disorders: What is the importance of the quality of the therapeutic alliance for outcomes? *Counselling Psychology Review*, 28(4), 34–46.

Berger, M., Wagner, T. H., & Baker, L. C. (2005). Internet use and stigmatized illness. *Social Science & Medicine*, 61(8), 1821–1827.

Bland, R. C., Newman, S. C., & Orn, H. (1997). Help-seeking for psychiatric disorders. *The Canadian Journal of Psychiatry/La Revue canadienne de psychiatrie*, 42, 935–42.

Breunlin, D. C. (1999). Toward a theory of constraints. *Journal of Marriage and Family Therapy*, 25(3): 365–382.

Button, E. J., Marshall, P., Shinkwin, R., Black, S. H., & Palmer, R. L. (1997). One hundred referrals to an eating disorders service: Progress and service consumption over a 2–4 year period. *European Eating Disorders Review*, 5(1), 47–63.

Carlat, D. J. & Camargo Jr., C. A. (1991). Review of bulimia nervosa in males. *The American Journal of Psychiatry*, 148(7), 831–843.

Cialdini, R. B. & Trost, M. R. (1999). Social influence: Social norms, conformity, and compliance. In D. Gilbert, S. Fiske, & G. Lindzy (Eds.), *The handbook of social psychology* (Vol. 2, pp. 151–192). Boston, MA: McGraw-Hill.

Claes, L., Jiménez-Murcia, S., Agüera, Z., Castro, R., Sánchez, I., Menchón, J. M., & Fernández-Aranda, F. (2012). Male eating disorder patients with and without non-suicidal self-injury: A comparison of psychopathological and personality features. *European Eating Disorders Review, 20*(4), 335–338.

Cockell, S. J., Geller, J., & Linden, W. (2003). Decisional balance in anorexia nervosa: Capitalizing on ambivalence. *European Eating Disorders Review, 11*(2), 75–89.

Colton, A. & Pistrang, N. (2004). Adolescents' experiences of inpatient treatment for anorexia nervosa. *European Eating Disorders Review, 12*(5), 307–316.

Crowther, J. H. & Sherwood, N. E. (1997). Assessment. In D. M. Garner & P. E. Garfinkel (Eds.), *Handbook of treatment for eating disorders* (2nd ed.). New York: The Guilford Press.

Darcy, A. M. & Lin, I. H. J. (2013). Are we asking the right questions? A review of assessment of males with eating disorders. In L. Cohn & R. Lemberg (Eds.), *Current findings on males with eating disorders.* (pp. 4–10). New York: Routledge.

Darcy, A.M., Katz, S., Fitzpatrick, K.K., Forsberg, S., Utzinger, L., & Lock, J. (2010). All better? How former anorexia nervosa patients define recovery and engaged in treatment. *European Eating Disorders Review, 18*(4), 260–270.

David, D. S. & Brannon, R. (Eds.) (1976). *The forty-nine percent majority: The male sex role.* Reading, MA: Addison Wesley Publishing Company.

Elvins, R. & Green, J. (2008). The conceptualization and measurement of therapeutic alliance: An empirical review. *Clinical Psychology Review, 28*(7), 1167–1187.

Fairburn, C. G. & Gowers, S. G. (2008). Eating disorders. In M. Rutter, D. Bishop, D. Pine, S. Scott, J. Stevenson, E. Taylor, & A. Thapar (Eds.), *Rutter's child and adolescent psychiatry,* (pp. 670–685). Oxford: Blackwell.

Fairburn, C. G. & Harrison, P. J. (2003). Eating disorders. *The Lancet, 361*(9355), 407–416.

Forsberg, S., LoTempio, E., Bryson, S., Fitzpatrick, K. K., le Grange, D., & Lock, J. (2014). Parent–therapist alliance in family-based treatment for adolescents with anorexia nervosa. *European Eating Disorders Review, 22*(1), 53–58.

Galdas, P. M., Cheater, F., & Marshall, P. (2005). Men and health help-seeking behaviour: Literature review. *Journal of Advanced Nursing, 49*(6), 616–623.

Garner, D. M. & Bemis, K. M. (1982). A cognitive-behavioral approach to anorexia nervosa. *Cognitive Therapy and Research, 6*(2), 123–150.

Garner, D. M., Vitousek, K. M., & Pike, K. M. (1997). Cognitive-behavioral therapy for anorexia nervosa. In D. M. Garner & P. E. Garfinkel (Eds.), *Handbook of treatment for eating disorders* (2nd ed.). New York: The Guilford Press.

Good, G. & Wood, P. (1995). Male gender role conflict, depression, and help seeking: Do college men face double jeopardy? *Journal of Counseling and Development, 74,* 70–75.

Gueguen, J., Godart, N., Chambry, J., Brun-Eberentz, A., Foulon, C., Snezana, M., ... & Huas, C. (2012). Severe anorexia nervosa in men: Comparison with severe AN in women and analysis of mortality. *International Journal of Eating Disorders, 45*(4), 537–545.

Hammer, J., Vogel, D., & Heimerdinger-Edwards, S. (2013). Men's help seeking: Examination of differences across community size, education, and income. *Psychology of Men and Masculinity, 14*, 65–75.

Hildebrandt, T., Lai, J. K., Langenbucher, J. W., Schneider, M., Yehuda, R., & Pfaff, D. W. (2011). The diagnostic dilemma of pathological appearance and performance enhancing drug use. *Drug and Alcohol Dependence, 114*(1), 1–11.

Jennings, K. S., Cheung, J. H., Britt, T. W., Goguen, K. N., Jeffirs, S. M., Peasley, A. L., & Lee, A. C. (2015). How are perceived stigma, self-stigma, and self-reliance related to treatment-seeking? A three-path model. *Psychiatric Rehabilitation Journal, 38*(2), 109–16.

Keel, P. K. & McCormick, L. (2010). Diagnosis, assessment, and treatment planning for anorexia nervosa. In C. M. Grillo & J. E. Mitchell (Eds.) *The treatment of eating disorders: A clinical handbook,* (pp. 3–27). New York: Guilford Press.

Keys, A., Brozek, J., Henschel, A., & Mickelson, O. & Taylor, H. L. (1950). *The biology of human starvation.* Vols. I–II. Minneaopolis, MN: University of Minnesota Press.

Lask, B. & Hage, T. W. (2013). Therapeutic engagement. In R. Bryant-Waugh & B. Lask (Eds.), *Eating disorders in childhood and adolescence* (4th ed. pp. 197–221). New York: Routledge.

Mahalik, J. R. (2000). Men's gender role conflict as predictors of self-ratings on the Interpersonal Circle. *Journal of Social and Clinical Psychology, 19*, 276–292.

Margolis, R. L., Spencer, W., Depaulo, J. R., Simpson, S. G., & Andersen, A. E. (1994). Psychiatric comorbidity in subgroups of eating-disordered inpatients. *Eating Disorders, 2*(3), 231–236.

Mitchell, J. & Peterson, C. (Eds.) (2007). *Assessment of eating disorders.* New York: The Guilford Press.

Murray, S. B., Rieger, E., Hildebrandt, T., Karlov, L., Russell, J., Boon, E., ... & Touyz, S. W. (2012). A comparison of eating, exercise, shape, and weight related symptomatology in males with muscle dysmorphia and anorexia nervosa. *Body Image, 9*(2), 193–200.

Nadler, A. (1990). Help-seeking behavior as a coping resource. In M. Rosenbaum (Ed.), *Learned resourcefulness: On coping skills, self-control, and adaptive behavior* (pp. 127–162). New York: Springer.

Nicholson, L. (2013). *Feminism/postmodernism.* New York: Routledge.

Norcross, J. C., Krebs, P. M., & Prochaska, J. O. (2011). Stages of change. *Journal of Clinical Psychology, 67*, 143–154.

Parkinson, K. N., Tovée, M. J., & Cohen-Tovée, E. M. (1998). Body shape perceptions of preadolescent and young adolescent children. *European Eating Disorders Review, 6*(2), 126–135.

Pereira, T., Lock, J., & Oggins, J. (2006). Role of therapeutic alliance in family therapy for adolescent anorexia nervosa. *International Journal of Eating Disorders, 39*(8), 677–684.

Pike, K. M., Loeb, K., & Vitousek, K. (1996). Cognitive-behavioral therapy for anorexia nervosa and bulimia nervosa. In J. K. Thompson (Ed.), *Body image: Eating disorders and obesity,* (pp. 253–302). Washington, DC: American Psychological Association.

Pinsof, W.M. (1995). *Integrative problem-centered therapy: A synthesis of family, individual, and biological therapies.* New York: Basic Books.

Pope, H. G., Katz, D. L., & Hudson, J. I. (1993). Anorexia nervosa and "reverse anorexia" among 108 male bodybuilders. *Comprehensive Psychiatry*, *34*(6), 406–409.

Prochaska, J. O. (1999). Change at differing stages. In C. Snyder & R. Ingram (Eds.), *Handbook of psychological change*. New York: John Wiley.

Raevuori, A., Keski-Rahkonen, A., & Hoek, H. W. (2014). A review of eating disorders in males. *Current Opinion in Psychiatry*, *27*(6), 426–430.

Räisänen, U. & Hunt, K. (2014). The role of gendered constructions of eating disorders in delayed help-seeking in men: A qualitative interview study. *British Medical Journal Open*, *4*(4) e004342, doi: 10.1136/bmjopen-2013-004342.

Reid, M., Burr, J., Williams, S., & Hammersley, R. (2008). Eating disorders patients' views on their disorders and on an outpatient service: A qualitative study. *Journal of Health Psychology*, *13*(7), 956–960.

Rich, E. (2006). Anorexic dis(connection): Managing anorexia as an illness and an identity. *Sociology of Health & Illness*, *28*(30), 284–305.

Robertson, J. M. & Fitzgerald, L. F. (1992). Overcoming the masculine mystique: Preferences for alternative forms of assistance among men who avoid counseling. *Journal of Counseling Psychology*, *39*(2), 240–246.

Runfola, C. D., Allison, K. C., Hardy, K. K., Lock, J., & Peebles, R. (2014). Prevalence and clinical significance of night eating syndrome in university students. *Journal of Adolescent Health*, *55*(1), 41–48.

Satcher, D. (1999). Mental health: A report of the surgeon general. Retrieved September 14, 2007, from http://www.surgeongeneral.gov/library/mentalhealth/home.html.

Scheff, T. (2014). Toward a concept of stigma. *International Journal of Social Psychiatry*, *60*(7), 724–725.

Sly, R. (2009). What's in a name? Classifying "the dropout" from treatment for anorexia nervosa. *European Eating Disorders Review*, *17*(6), 405–407.

Sly, R., Morgan, J. F., Mountford, V. A., & Lacey, J. H. (2013). Predicting premature termination of hospitalised treatment for anorexia nervosa: The roles of therapeutic alliance, motivation, and behaviour change. *Eating Behaviors*, *14*(2), 119–123.

Sly, R., Morgan, J. F., Mountford, V. A., Sawer, F., Evans, C., & Lacey, J. H. (2014). Rules of engagement: Qualitative experiences of therapeutic alliance when receiving in-patient treatment for anorexia nervosa. *Eating Disorders*, *22*(3), 233–243.

Smink, F. R., van Hoeken, D., & Hoek, H. W. (2012). Epidemiology of eating disorders: Incidence, prevalence and mortality rates. *Current Psychiatry Reports*, *14*(4), 406–414.

Smith, A. T., Kelly-Weeder, S., Engel, J., McGowan, K. A., Anderson, B., & Wolfe, B. E. (2011). Quality of eating disorder websites: What adolescents and their families need to know. *Journal of Child and Psychiatric Nursing*, *24*, 33–37.

Sparks, J. A., Duncan, B. L., & Miller, S. D. (2008). Common factors in psychotherapy. In. J. L. Lebow (Ed.), *Twenty-first century psychotherapies: Contemporary approaches to theory and practice* (pp. 453–497). New York: John Wiley

Stice, E. (2002). Risk and maintenance factors for eating pathology: A meta-analytic review. *Psychological Bulletin*, *128*(5), 825–848.

Swanson, S. A., Crow, S. J., le Grange, D., Swendsen, J., & Merikangas, K. R. (2011). Prevalence and correlates of eating disorders in adolescents: Results from the national comorbidity survey replication adolescent supplement. *Archives of General Psychiatry, 68*(7), 714–723.

Tholin, S., Lindroos, A., Tynelius, P., Stunkard, A. J., Bulik, C. M., & Rasmussen, F. (2009). Prevalence of night eating in obese and nonobese twins. *Obesity, 17*(5), 1050–1055.

Tierney, S. (2008). The individual within a condition: A qualitative study of young people's reflections on being treated for anorexia nervosa. *Journal of the American Psychiatric Nurses Association, 13*(6), 368–375.

Treasure, J. & Ward, A. (1997). A practical guide to the use of motivational interviewing in anorexia nervosa. *European Eating Disorders Review, 5*(2), 102–114.

Warin, M. (2004). Primitivising anorexia: The irresistible spectacle of not eating. *The Australian Journal of Anthropology, 15*(1), 95–104.

Williams, S. & Reid, M. (2010). Understanding the experience of ambivalence in anorexia nervosa: The maintainer's perspective. *Psychology & Health, 25*(5), 551–567.

Wollburg, E., Meyer, B., Osen, B., & Löwe, B. (2013). Psychological change mechanisms in anorexia nervosa treatments: How much do we know? *Journal of Clinical Psychology, 69*(7), 762–773.

4 The Systemic Metaframework

Mark, a 15-year-old boy with anorexia nervosa, and his mother, Lisa, and father, George, attended their first family psychotherapy appointment after being referred to me by their family doctor. During the first session, Lisa described her worries about Mark whereas George, in contrast, remained relatively silent. At one point early in the session, as we talked through her fears and worries about her son, Lisa began to cry profusely. For a few moments, as Lisa cried quietly, I wondered whether I ought to step in and comfort her. Before I could decide, though, Mark moved to the couch to sit next to his mother and said, "It's okay Mom. It's not your fault. Don't cry." Through the entire episode, George remained on the periphery, looking deeply uncomfortable.

After the family regained its equilibrium, I commented on Mark's ability to calm and comfort his mother, especially compared to father's "hands off" approach. I went on to note the high degree of closeness between mother and son, in contrast to the father's apparent distance from both. In making this observation, it was essential to remember that I did not know whether this family organization preceded the development of Mark's symptoms or, in fact, arose in response to stress the family was experiencing. Regardless, it was clear that the dynamic I was observing put inappropriate pressure on Mark to comfort his mother and, furthermore, deprived the family system of the emotional resources that George might have been able to provide.

The role of families in the understanding and treatment of anorexia nervosa is immense. With that in mind, in this chapter, we develop a metaframework that integrates family systems theories with an eye toward men and boys with the disorder. As the patient with anorexia nervosa withdraws further into a world centered on food restriction and weight loss, he withdraws from the world of relational connection. Unsurprisingly, the illness has a devastating impact on the families of the afflicted. Early in treatment, family and friends, and parents in particular, often struggle with denial and misinformation as well as shame and guilt as they begin to recognize the patient's struggles. As treatment begins, families must be engaged in the treatment process as a valuable resource and motivator for the patient. Indeed, systemic theories are clinically useful because they "broaden the symptom" by exploring the ways factors in the family system may constrain the resolution of the presenting problem (Pinsof, 1995, 2005). And throughout treatment, especially in later stages, families may struggle to understand, grieve, and forgive their own role in the disorder's development and maintenance.[1]

In the early stages of treatment, one of the foremost takes of engaging male patients in treatment involves addressing the stigma they face for suffering from a "woman's problem" (Andersen, Cohn, & Holbrook, 2000). While this is discussed extensively in Chapter 3: Diagnosis, Engagement, and Alliance, here it should be noted that families are an integral component of this process. During the engagement and alliance-building phase, it is hoped that families can be enlisted to, first, accept that men and boys do, in fact, suffer from anorexia nervosa and, second, to become advocates for the patient in the health care system.

In recent years, there has been a remarkable enthusiasm for family-based treatment of anorexia nervosa. Family-based treatments have been invaluable for highlighting the ways that families can be an immense resource for individuals with eating disorders. In fact, many researchers and clinicians are convinced that when weight restoration is the foremost priority of treatment, family-based therapy is the gold standard intervention (Lock & le Grange, 2015). As it turns out, family-based treatments have a long and complex history with patients with anorexia nervosa and their families.

Family Therapy and Anorexia Nervosa

The family systems approach to treatment began with the pioneering work in the 1950s that attempted to understand families with a schizophrenic member (Bateson, Jackson, Haley, & Weakland, 1956). These investigations suggested that families operated according to rules that dictated interpersonal behavior and communication. The family therapist's task, thus, was to challenge and disrupt these rules, which were seen as preventing the family from finding creative solutions to their problems. As part of this approach, it was recognized that the identified patient, or symptomatic family member, was expressing the problematic dynamics of the entire family.

Family therapists have been attempting to understand and intervene with the families of anorexic patients for many years (Selvini Palazzoli, 1974; Minuchin, Rosman, & Baker, 1978). In fact, it has been noted that anorexia nervosa has played an important role in the work of many influential members of the family therapy movement. The "anorexia family" became a paradigm for the development of the field of family therapy in much the same way hysteria was a cornerstone for Freud's development of psychoanalysis (Dare & Eisler, 1997).

Working with colleagues at the Philadelphia Child Guidance Clinic, Salvador Minuchin developed the "psychosomatic family model" of structural family therapy to explain his observations of patients with anorexia nervosa and their families. Using this model, Minuchin argued that patients develop anorexia nervosa and other psychosomatic illnesses through a conjunction of physiological vulnerability, shared family characteristics (which include enmeshment, overprotectiveness, rigidity, and lack of conflict resolution), and the reinforcement of the child's illness because it plays an important role in the family's avoidance of conflict (Minuchin et al., 1975). With this understanding as a guide, Minuchin's goal is to alter problematic aspects of family organization by limiting some patterns of interaction and encouraging others. The structural family therapy approach to treatment has notable empirical validation (Minuchin, Rosman, & Baker, 1978) and has been adapted by other approaches to family-based treatment (Russell, Szmukler, Dare, & Eisler, 1987; Dare, Eisler, Russell, & Szmukler, 1990).

The Milan approach is likely the second most influential model of family therapy for the treatment of eating disorders. This model holds that the family has become a rigidly organized interactional system and that anorexia nervosa has come to play an important role in maintaining the family's homeostasis (Selvini Palazzoli, 1974). Maintaining a neutral stance with regard to the family and, in fact, about whether change should occur at all, the clinician attempts to introduce a new perspective that broadens the family's understanding of the symptoms. This approach has received little empirical support, with only one investigation having been carried out (Stierlin & Weber, 1989).

While not prescribing specific interventions, the feminist critique of family therapy has often been applied to the treatment of anorexia nervosa. This approach has made at least two important contributions to the treatment of the disorder. First, it recognizes the inequitable position of women in society, which includes (1) the expectation that women should be nurturers and caretakers and (2) demands adherence to culturally defined norms of physical attraction (Dare & Eisler, 1997). The feminist critique recognizes that these factors are internalized in patients with anorexia nervosa (Orbach, 1979). Indeed, the feminist critique is invaluable for casting light on the impact of role expectations and cultural demands on women and girls. In this book, we hope to emphasize that men and boys, too, are subject to unique expectations and demands. This is discussed throughout the book and particularly in Chapter 6: The Culture and Gender Metaframework.

The Maudsley approach adopts an interactional systems model to understand the multifactorial etiology of anorexia nervosa (Dare & Eisler, 1997). While genetic, sociocultural, and familial factors may contribute to the symptoms, the symptoms also have an enormous impact on the functioning of the family and the individual. Indeed, it is likely that some of the pathological factors observed in both the individual patient and his family are not antecedent to the disorder's development but a consequence of it.[2] This approach to treatment has garnered extensive empirical support suggesting, for example, that adolescents with short duration anorexia nervosa respond well to family therapy both in the short term and at later follow-up (Russell, Szmukler, Dare, & Eisler, 1987; Dare, Eisler, Russell & Szmukler, 1990). Similarly, evidence supports the approach for adult patients whose illness began in adolescence (Russell, Dare, Eisler, & le Grange, 1992).

The Maudsley approach is notable for its "agnostic" view of the parents' involvement in the child's illness (Eisler, 1995). While differentiating itself from psychoanalytic thinking in many ways, the pioneers of family therapy often joined with that thinking in emphasizing psychopathology in the parents' relationship with the child and the mother–child relationship in particular. In its attempts to involve peripheral fathers and provide space between overinvolved mothers and children, structural family therapy, for example, often seems to imply that the real problem lies in the parents' relationship with their child (Dare & Eisler, 1997). Taking an agnostic view is supported by the observation that higher levels of criticism negatively impact the treatment process and outcome for patients with anorexia nervosa (Szmukler, Eisler, Russell, & Dare, 1985).

My own view of this problem is complex. While a strictly agnostic approach, which does not assume that parents are in any way responsible for their child's illness, is most appropriate at the beginning of treatment, there must also be room, at the appropriate time, for the patient system to begin to sort out the contribution of various members in the arising and maintenance of the disorder. The complete resolution of anorexia nervosa involves not just weight restoration and correction of problematic attitudes about food, weight, and shape but, equally important, the development of a clear understanding of factors that gave rise to and maintained the problem. In this process, there is often considerable grief and regret, which must be distinguished from anger and blame.

The integrative approach presented in this book is aligned with this view. It makes no assumptions about the etiology of the disorder. Instead, treatment is intended to recognize and lift the unique web of constraints that accompanies each patient system. In fact, in terms of treatment intervention, causality is not relevant. Ultimately, the presence of familial factors that constrain problem resolution should not lead treatment providers to pathologize families but, instead, to include them in the direct patient system when appropriate. Yet we must also recognize that it is natural for family and friends to struggle with the question of why the patient developed a psychological illness. In my view, clinicians must acknowledge this struggle. With appropriate support, families often begin to think through their own role in the disorder's development and maintenance. If appropriate, there may be a period of mourning and forgiveness that takes place within the family. And if families struggle in this process, constraints that impede mourning and forgiveness become aspects of the problem-maintenance space to be resolved during treatment. Forgiveness is discussed in Chapter 9: The Spiritual Metaframework.

Empirical Research on Families

Knowledge about the organization of families of individuals with anorexia nervosa has a significant impact on prevention and treatment (Eagles, Johnston, & Millar, 2005). With this in mind, we now turn to empirical research on families with a member who struggles with anorexia nervosa. In reviewing this literature, we focus specifically on families of men and boys who suffer from the disorder. Indeed, family environment has been shown to be a significant risk factor for the development of anorexia nervosa in both adolescent boys and girls (Felker & Stivers, 1994). Because our first exposure to the social aspects of eating habits and disturbances is in the family, it is unsurprising that certain factors in the family are tied to the development and maintenance of the disorder

Little is known about the demographic characteristics of families of men and boys with anorexia nervosa. At present, while no link has been found between anorexia nervosa and birth order, number of siblings, or sex of siblings (Gowers, Kadambari, & Crisp, 1985), males with anorexia nervosa may be more likely to live or have grown up in a single parent home (Lindblad, Lindberg, & Hjern, 2006) or to have fathers who live separately or have died (Nelson, Hughes, Katz, & Searight, 1999). This latter observation may be supported by the finding that femininity may be associated with higher levels of eating psychopathology than masculinity (Meyer, Blissett & Oldfield, 2001; Cotrufo, Cella, Cremato, & Labella, 2007) and that boys and men with anorexia nervosa see themselves and are seen by others as more feminine than other males (Fitcher & Daser, 1987). For some boys with the disorder, the lack of a father with whom to identify, combined with an overly involved mother–son relationship (Romero, 1994), may block a fuller expression of masculine identity and, thus, increase the risk of anorexia nervosa developing.

Organizational factors make up another important theoretical approach encompassed in the family systems metaframework. Also called family interactions (Fishman, 2005), this component addresses how the patient system organizes and conducts itself in regard to the presenting problem. Its primary concern is boundaries, the rules that determine how members of the patient system relate to each other (Pinsof, 1995). Depending on the family systems model, family interactions can be as specific as certain behaviors (e.g., teasing) or as broad as abstract ideas like conflict and intimacy.

Past research on organizational factors has focused on the mother–daughter relationship to the exclusion of fathers and sons. Research suggests, for example, that mothers of girls with anorexia nervosa report high levels of concern and over-control, and may also convey inappropriate or inconsistent messages about self-regulation and age-appropriate autonomy. However, knowledge about the interactions of all family members – including the roles of fathers and sons in the family – may reveal important information (May, Kim, McHale, & Crouter, 2006) and demands further research.

Felker and Stivers (1994) examined abstract differences in the family interactions of adolescent boys and girls with anorexia nervosa. Consistent with previous research, family environment was shown to be a significant risk factor for the development of the disorder. With regard to adolescent boys, several patterns of interaction were shown to be predictive, such as less independence and autonomy. Supporting this finding, Romero (1994) reported that many mothers of males with anorexia nervosa are overly controlling and protective. Because boys with controlling and protective mothers lack the experience necessary to gain confidence for self-initiated behavior, they are unable to cope with the demands of adolescence. As a result, the boys' independence is compromised and the development of that independence may be an important goal in treatment.

Felker and Stivers (1994) also reported that greater conflict, control, and achievement orientation were linked with risk for developing the disorder. In support of this idea, Sterling and Segal (1985) reported strong indications of excessive parental expectations for these male children. In another study, several males stated that their fathers pressured them to excel in sports or to have a muscular physique (Romero, 1994). Here, treatment may focus on helping boys to develop a broader-based self-esteem and to rework ideals and aspirations in both the patient and the parental subsystem.

There is also research that examines the link between family organization and weight concern in men and boys. Unsurprisingly, extensive research demonstrates that excessive weight concern is linked with the development of anorexia nervosa (e.g., Killen et al., 1996). As a result, family interactions that are linked with weight concern are indirectly linked to the development of the disorder.

Research suggests that adolescent girls' weight concerns increase over time with a peak at age 16, after which they began to decline. In contrast, adolescent boys' weight concerns are similar to girls at age 11 but decline throughout adolescence (May, Kim, McHale, & Crouter, 2006). This finding is supported by the fact that puberty is a greater risk factor for girls than boys. As discussed in Chapter 5: The Biological Metaframework, girls experience a larger increase in fat relative to muscle than boys (Crisp & Burns 1990). In addition, conflict with mothers and fathers is correlated with weight concern; indeed, parent–adolescent conflict may be the most important relationship quality linked to weight concern (May, Kim, McHale, & Crouter, 2006) and, thus, reduction of this conflict may be an important aspect of successful treatment.

What can be said about the intergenerational aspects of family systems? There is evidence that first-degree relatives with anorexia nervosa are a significant risk factor for adolescent boys developing the disorder. In one study, 13.8 percent of families of male patients with anorexia nervosa had at least one relative with the disorder (Strober, Freeman, Lampert, Diamond, & Kaye, 2000). While this is consistent with the idea that genetics predisposes individuals to developing anorexia nervosa (Bulik, Slof-Op'T Landt, van Furth, & Sullivan, 2007), treatment providers should explore how families have understood the relative's illness and the impact, if any, it continues to have on the patient system.

Mark, Lisa, and George

Through the process of family therapy, in sessions with the parental subsystem, Lisa, George, and I explored the importance of strengthening their alliance and taking charge of Mark's eating and health. In the process, the couple was forced to confront long-standing conflicts in their marriage that had previously been overlooked. In the early stages of this process, I took a relatively directive approach in an attempt to model the authority and structure that Lisa and George needed with their son, Mark.

THERAPIST: You've been working with the nutritionist to help Mark get his weight up. And from what I understand, it's been hard to get Mark to eat his meals…

LISA: You know, I feel like I'm in this alone. George doesn't back me up. Mark says he's not going to eat, and then what am I supposed to do? I end up begging him, and he takes a bite or two.

THERAPIST: George, I'm wondering what comes up for you in the process…

GEORGE: You know, Lisa doesn't ask for help. I could help! But when I try to help, she tells me I'm messing it up – always there's something wrong. I fix that thing, and then it's something else that's wrong.

THERAPIST: Lisa, what I'm hearing is that you'd like your husband to help, but you feel he doesn't show up. George, what I'm hearing from you is that you'd like to help, but that you feel criticized and shut out. It seems that, at least in part, you're both after the same thing here.

In this excerpt, I am working with the parental subsystem in an effort to increase collaboration so that they can assume the authority required to facilitate the nutritional rehabilitation of their son, Mark. Although this was a long and difficult process, the couple was able to address their conflicts in the protected space of family therapy while increasingly operating as a team in the family situation. Ultimately, I referred Lisa and George to a couples therapist so that they could begin to address the long-avoided conflicts in their marriage, many of which undermined their attempts to parent together.

Because Lisa was increasingly able to rely on George for comfort and support, Mark was able, with the support of his individual psychotherapist, to move into a position of greater individuation. He was able to acknowledge and act from his own desire to improve his physical and psychological health. While Mark's increasing independence in the later stages of treatment was often difficult for Lisa, who felt she was losing her son, George was often able both to coach his wife through these moments and to provide his son with needed encouragement.

In the following chapter, we develop a biological metaframework. Anorexia nervosa is deeply intertwined with the body and its processes and manifests, at the biological level, differently in men and boys than in women and girls. In this chapter, we discuss the role of genetic vulnerability in the disorder as well as the importance of full nutritional rehabilitation. We then turn to the medical complications that often arise, including dermatological, gastrointestinal, cardiovascular, and endocrine problems as well as considerations regarding refeeding syndrome. Finally, we consider the male pubertal process and its implications for the development of anorexia nervosa in adolescent boys.

Notes

1 Because of the severity of the disorder that brings men and boys with anorexia nervosa to treatment, it is especially difficult to pull apart cause and effect in family dynamics (Sterling & Segal, 1985). This should give us pause in making causal explanations with regard to pathological behavior in families.
2 For example, as the illness proceeds entire families often become enmeshed in the anorexic patient's dieting practices and food restrictions (Beumont, Beumont, Touyz, & Williams, 1997). In many cases, this dynamic was not present before the disorder developed.

References

Andersen, A. E., Cohn, L., & Holbrook, T. (2000). *Making weight: Healing men's conflicts with food, weight, and shape.* Carlsbad, CA: Gürze Books.
Bateson, G., Jackson, D. D., Haley, J., & Weakland, J. (1956). Toward a theory of schizophrenia. *Behavioral Science, 1,* 251–264.
Beumont, P. J., Beumont, C. C., Touyz, S. W., & Williams, H. (1997). Nutritional counseling and supervised exercise. In D. M. Garner & P. E. Garfinkel (Eds.).,*Handbook of treatment for eating disorders* (pp. 178–187). New York: Guilford.
Bulik, C. M., Slof-Op'T Landt, M. C., van Furth, E. F., & Sullivan, P. F. (2007). The genetics of anorexia nervosa. *Annual Review of Nutrition, 27,* 263–275.

Cotrufo, P., Cella, S., Cremato, F., & Labella, A. G. (2007). Eating disorder attitude and abnormal eating behaviours in a sample of 11–13-year old school children: The role of pubertal body transformation. *Eating and Weight Disorders – Studies on Anorexia, Bulimia, and Obesity, 12*(4), 154–160.

Crisp, A. H. & Burns, T. (1990). Primary anorexia nervosa in the male and female: A comparison of clinical features and prognosis. In A. E. Andersen (Ed.), *Males with eating disorders* (pp. 77–99). New York: Brunner/Mazel.

Dare, C. & Eisler, I. (1997). Family therapy for anorexia nervosa. In D. M. Garner & P. E. Garfinkel (Eds.). *Handbook of treatment for eating disorders* (2nd ed.). New York: The Guilford Press.

Dare, C., Eisler, I., Russell, G. F., & Szmukler, G. I. (1990). The clinical and theoretical impact of a controlled trial of family therapy in anorexia nervosa. *Journal of Marital and Family Therapy, 16*(1), 39–57.

Eagles, J. M., Johnston, M. I., & Millar, H. R. (2005). A case-control study of family composition in anorexia nervosa. *International Journal of Eating Disorders, 38*(1), 49–54.

Eisler, I. (1995). Family models of eating disorders. In G. Szmukler, C. Dare, & J. Treasure (Eds.), *Handbook of eating disorders: Theory, treatment, and research* (pp. 155–176). Chichester: John Wiley & Sons.

Felker, K. R. & Stivers, C. (1994). The relationship of gender and family environment to eating disorder risk in adolescents. *Adolescence, 29*(116), 821–834.

Fishman, H. C. (2005). *Enduring change in eating disorders: Interventions with long-term results*. New York: Routledge.

Fitcher, M. M. & Daser, C. (1987). Symptomatology, psychosexual development, and gender identity in 42 anorexic males. *Psychological Medicine, 17,* 409–418.

Gowers, S., Kadambari, S. R., & Crisp, A. H. (1985). Family structure and birth order of patients with anorexia nervosa. *Journal of Psychiatric Research, 19*(2), 247–251.

Killen, J. D., Taylor, C. B., Hayward, C., Haydel, K. F., Wilson, D. M., Hammer, L., ... & Strachowski, D. (1996). Weight concerns influence the development of eating disorders: A 4-year prospective study. *Journal of Consulting and Clinical Psychology, 64*(5), 936–940.

Lindblad, F., Lindberg, L., & Hjern, A. (2006). Anorexia nervosa in young men: A cohort study. *International Journal of Eating Disorders, 39*(8), 662–666.

Lock, J. & le Grange, D. (2015). *Treatment manual for anorexia nervosa: A family-based approach*. New York: Guilford Publications.

May, A. L., Kim, J., McHale, S. M., & Crouter, A. C. (2006). Parent-adolescent relationships and the development of weight concerns from early to late adolescence. *International Journal of Eating Disorders, 39*(8), 729–740.

Meyer, C., Blissett, J., & Oldfield, C. (2001). Sexual orientation and eating psychopathology: The role of masculinity and femininity. *International Journal of Eating Disorders, 29*(3), 314–318.

Minuchin, S., Baker, L., Rosman, B. L., Liebman, R., Milman, L., & Todd, T. C. (1975). A conceptual model of psychosomatic illness in children: Family organization and family therapy. *Archives of General Psychiatry, 32*(8), 1031–1038.

Minuchin, S., Rosman, B. L., & Baker, L. (1978). *Psychosomatic families: Anorexia nervosa in context*. Cambridge, MA; Harvard University Press.

Nelson, W. L., Hughes, H. M., Katz, B., & Searight, H. R. (1999). Anorexic eating attitudes and behaviors of male and female college students. *Adolescence*, *34*(135), 621–633.

Orbach, S. (1979). *Fat is a feminist issue*. New YorK: Arrow Books.

Pinsof, W. M. (1995). *Integrative problem-centered therapy: A synthesis of family, individual, and biological therapies*. New York: Basic Books.

Pinsof, W. M. (2005). Integrative problem-centered therapy. In J. C. Norcross & M. R. Goldfried (Eds.), *Handbook of psychotherapy integration* (pp. 282–402). Oxford University Press

Romero, F. (1994). Adolescent boys and anorexia nervosa. *Adolescence*, *29*(115), 643–647.

Russell, G. F., Szmukler, G. I., Dare, C., & Eisler, I. (1987). An evaluation of family therapy in anorexia nervosa and bulimia nervosa. *Archives of General Psychiatry*, *44*(12), 1047–1056.

Russell, G. F. M., Dare, C., Eisler, I., & le Grange, D. (1992). Controlled trials of family treatments in anorexia nervosa. In K. A Halmi (Ed.), *Psychobiology and treatment of anorexia nervosa and bulimia nervosa* (pp. 237–261). Arlington, VA: American Psychiatric Press.

Selvini Palazzoli, M. (1974). *Self-starvation*. London: Chaucer.

Sterling, J. W. & Segal, J. D. (1985). Anorexia nervosa in males: A critical review. *International Journal of Eating Disorders, 4*(4), 559–572.

Stierlin, H., & Weber, G. (1989). *Unlocking the family door: A systemic approach to the understanding and treatment of anorexia nervosa*. New York: Brunner/Mazel.

Strober, M., Freeman, R., Lampert, C., Diamond, J., & Kaye, W. (2000). Controlled family study of anorexia nervosa and bulimia nervosa: Evidence of shared liability and transmission of partial syndromes. *American Journal of Psychiatry*, *157*(3), 393–401.

Szmukler, G. I., Eisler, I., Russell, G. F., & Dare, C. (1985). Anorexia nervosa, parental "expressed emotion" and dropping out of treatment. *The British Journal of Psychiatry*, *147*(3), 265–271.

5 The Biological Metaframework

Roberto, a 16-year-old boy, came to treatment with his mother, Lisa, after she found his hair in the shower drain. With growing concern, Lisa spoke with a family friend, who happened to be a therapist, and the friend recommended she seek treatment for her son immediately. During the first session, I learned that Roberto had been teased by a cross-country teammate for his "tubby" stomach and, since that time, had endeavored to achieve a firm definition of his abdominal muscles. Most notable in the initial interview was the perseverative quality of Roberto's thinking, represented by his tendency to become overly focused on specific facts – for example, caloric intake and weight.

After an initial consultation, I referred Roberto for a full medical evaluation. Roberto was 5 feet 10 inches tall with a weight of 125 lbs. A thorough laboratory panel showed that his endocrine hormone levels (testosterone, LSH, FSH) were significantly low and his potassium levels were below expected. In addition, Roberto reported severe problems with constipation and bloating, stating that his stomach "feels huge." Roberto's mother noted that her son was more tired than usual.

As this brief vignette illustrates, anorexia nervosa is intimately linked to the body and its physical processes. Although it would be an error to approach formulation and treatment from a purely biological point of view, as symptoms and weight restriction are always linked with constraints on other levels of the problem-maintenance space, it would be equally problematic to neglect the complex web of constraints that always exists at the biological level of the problem-maintenance space.

With this in mind, in this chapter we develop a metaframework intended to capture important information about the biological aspects of anorexia nervosa in males. After discussing the role of genetic vulnerability in the disorder and the importance of attending to full nutritional rehabilitation, we take up the medical complications encountered in the treatment process. Although this topic has been comprehensively addressed in other sources (Mehler, Birmingham, Crow, & Jahraus, 2010), we approach the topic with an eye toward the clinical presentation and medical complications of male patients, which include dermatological, gastrointestinal, cardiovascular, and endocrine problems as well as considerations regarding refeeding syndrome. We also discuss the complexities of the male pubertal process – in particular, the relationship between early and rapid puberty and premorbid overweight – and the implications of this for the development of anorexia nervosa in adolescent boys.

The Role of Genetics

One compelling line of research suggests that the genetic vulnerability to an eating disorder ranges from 50 to 70 percent. Indeed, monozygotic twins share a 50 percent chance of having an eating disorder if one is afflicted (Bulik et al., 2006). In this research, however, there is no conclusion as to what is being transmitted for genetic vulnerability. Indeed, this vulnerability could consist of a range of factors, whether biologically based difficulties with early feeding, a tendency to negative affect, or other factors related to temperament.

In an effort to reduce stigma and blame, many clinicians have adopted the view that anorexia nervosa develops almost entirely due to genetic factors. In our enthusiasm for medical research, we have given the complex web of factors that contribute to an eating disorder less attention than they deserve in both our conceptualizations and interventions. In part, this enthusiasm for biological explanation can be attributed to the intense anger and blame that was leveled at caregivers, mothers in particular, largely fueled by psychological theorizing of the 1960s and 1970s. These explanations, which tended to attribute the development of anorexia nervosa almost exclusively to pathological factors in the mother–child relationship, were overly simplistic and caused harm by inducing unnecessary shame and guilt in parents. In reaction to this, at present we have exchanged vilification of the mother for an often overly simplistic understanding of the complex developmental sequences implicated in psychological disorders such as anorexia nervosa.

Ultimately, I agree with Andersen (2014) that the quest for a purely biological explanation of eating disorders is an elusive one. Even when a specific gene is recognized, the metabolic steps from the gene to clinical manifestation of the illness must be identified. These steps are intertwined with the familial and cultural environment of the developing child. To verify this claim, we need only note that the prevalence of eating disorders is significantly larger in Westernized societies valuing slimness and in upper socioeconomic classes in developing countries (Mehler & Andersen, 1999).

Nutritional Rehabilitation

The physical, as well as some of the psychological, symptoms associated with anorexia nervosa are secondary to disturbances in nutrition (Beumont,

Beumont, Touyz, & Williams, 1997). In addition, sound nutrition encompasses far more than "normal" weight. Indeed, weight restoration alone does not mean that disturbances in eating behavior and attitudes are resolved. In many cases, problematic eating behaviors persist long after weight restoration, with continued impact on physical and psychological health (Windauer, Lennerts, Talbot, Touyz, & Beumont, 1993). Because of this, it is essential to attend to the full nutritional rehabilitation of patients with the disorder, which includes weight restoration as well as reestablishing healthy attitudes and behaviors.

Starvation deeply impacts our physical and psychological functioning. This is illustrated by the classic Keys study conducted on conscientious objectors during World War II (Keys, Brozek, Henschel, Mickelson, & Taylor, 1950). In this study, male subjects began in good physical and psychological health. After six months of consuming half their normal food intake, they developed a number of symptoms. Psychologically, they began to exhibit labile mood as well as anxiety, depression, apathy, low self-esteem, significant cognitive dysfunction, social withdrawal accompanied by disturbance in interpersonal functioning, and obsessive and ritualized behaviors, especially with regard to food and eating. Physically, they developed a variety of symptoms associated with anorexia nervosa, including hair loss, gastrointestinal problems, lowered body temperature, and changes in heart rate and metabolism. As this experiment indicates, starvation creates innumerable psychological and physical difficulties.

Patients with anorexia nervosa often begin their disorder by following popular weight loss practices promoted by the mass media, family, and friends (Beumont, Beumont, Touyz, & Williams, 1997). In my clinical experience, a number of male patients have adopted popular eating practices such as the Paleolithic or "caveman" diet, which may be more appealing to men and boys because of its masculine overtones. Others take up vegetarian or vegan diets, initially for diverse reasons. At times, in an attempt to avoid overt conflict or because of shared disturbances around food, weight, and shape, the entire family may become enmeshed in the patient's eating practices.

Patients often begin their diets by decreasing the consumption of foods containing simple sugars and fats, eventually avoiding these entirely. Similarly, patients show a preference for low-fat dairy products in favor of whole milk ones and avoidance of red meat is common. In addition to the narrowing of acceptable foods over time, patients also show changes in meal pattern and frequency, first eliminating snacks and, later, entire meals (Beumont, Beumont, Touyz, & Williams, 1997).

During the early stages of treatment, a registered dietician was engaged as part of the treatment team for Roberto and his family. In collaboration with other members of the team, the dietician helped Roberto to identify the ways in which his early attempts at "getting a six pack abs" by eating protein rich foods and neglecting fat and carbohydrate failed to account for his body's nutritional needs. Through educational interventions provided to both Roberto and his family as well guidance in meal planning, Roberto was increasingly able to move toward balanced eating. As nutritional rehabilitation proceeded, I observed a significant decrease in the perseverative quality of Roberto's thinking and, over time, we were able to explore his thoughts and feelings about food as well as a wide range of other topics in a new and more productive way.

Medical Complications

As treatment unfolded, I learned that Roberto's diagnosis had been preceded by several visits to his family physician, where he reported ongoing stomach pain that had been diagnosed as "irritable bowel syndrome." His decreasing weight and disturbances in the amount and frequency of meals had not been accounted for in this diagnosis. It was only when Roberto's mother, Lisa, had noticed his thinning hair and had spoken with a family friend that an appropriate referral was made. After a thorough medical evaluation, several other medical difficulties were noted, including a disturbance in endocrine hormones and low blood pressure.

Biological factors must be comprehensively addressed for treatment to be successful. Indeed, eating disorders are, along with HIV/AIDs, one of the "great pretenders" of our time, appearing in primary care physician's offices in many disguised forms. As Mehler and Andersen (1999) point out, a "rule out" approach, which focuses on all possible medical causes before accounting for changes in emotional state, to the diagnosis of eating disorders leads to treatment delay and worsening of symptoms. In fact, while it is theoretically possible, it is extremely rare for a patient to have the core psychological symptoms of an eating disorder that, later, is revealed to be the result of an underlying medical condition. While medical conditions may drive restricted food intake, the fear of fatness and distortions in body image are psychological phenomena.

Men and boys with anorexia nervosa suffer from many of the same medical conditions as their female counterparts, including dermatological, gastrointestinal, cardiovascular, and endocrine problems as well as refeeding syndrome. Indeed, these complications have been extensively described in the literature as they pertain to female patients (Mehler, Birmingham, Crow, & Jahraus, 2010). Here, we provide a brief overview of these conditions with attention to recent research about how they manifest in male patients. Finally, we discuss the prominence of osteoporosis and osteopenia in patients with anorexia nervosa and special considerations for male patients.[1]

Patients with anorexia nervosa often present with thinning scalp hair and lanugo (soft, fine hair), most often on the face, arms, back, and legs (Yager & Andersen, 2005). The skin may exhibit a yellowish hue, carotodermia, resulting from excess ingestion of carotene containing foods (Mehler, Birmingham, Crow, & Jahraus, 2010). Frequently, patients show difficulties in temperature regulation (Yager & Andersen, 2005).

Dental problems are commonly observed, particularly the erosion of dental enamel and sensitivity to temperature in patients who purge (Milosevic, Brodie, & Slade, 1997). These complications are particularly common in patients who vomit, as the acidic contents of the stomach create sores in the lips, loss of enamel on the teeth, gingivitis, as well as atrophy of the salivary glands (Mehler & Andersen, 1999). For these reasons, as soon as possible, patients should be instructed to brush gently using fluoride toothpaste after purging and to use neutral pH mouthwashes to reduce oral acidity.

Patients with eating disorders commonly experience gastrointestinal symptoms. At times, these symptoms can become so severe that they interfere with psychological treatment. In addition, eating disorders may exacerbate pre-existing gastrointestinal conditions such as irritable bowel syndrome. Patients with anorexia nervosa report gastrointestinal symptoms that include bloating, a feeling of fullness, nausea, constipation, abdominal pain and distention (Mehler & Andersen, 1999). As weight is lost, gastric emptying slows down. As a result, bloating, especially after food intake, begins to occur. Additionally, patients begin to report constipation as weight loss continues (Mehler, Birmingham, Crow, & Jahraus, 2010). While gastroesophageal reflux, or heartburn, is often reported, it tends to improve over time during weight restoration (Mehler & Andersen, 1999).

With the highest morbidity rate of any psychiatric disorder, cardiovascular problems deserve special attention. With ongoing weight loss, the heart muscle shrinks, the volume of cardiac chambers is decreased, and cardiac mass and output drops. This leads to a reduced capacity for exercise, reduced blood pressure, and fatigue (Mehler & Andersen, 1999). Low heart rate, or sinus bradycardia, may be the most common medical complication found at initial assessment of males with anorexia nervosa (Norris et al., 2012). In addition, hypotension – systolic blood pressure less than 90 mm Hg and/or diastolic blood pressure less than 50 mm Hg – is often reported (Mehler, Birmingham, Crow, & Jahraus, 2010).

Anorexia nervosa causes significant endocrine disruption (Mehler, Birmingham, Crow, & Jahraus, 2010). While most research on endocrine disruption in anorexia nervosa focuses on amenorrhea in female patients as a manifestation of this disturbance, males with anorexia nervosa experience an equivalent degree of disruption (Herzog, Bradburn, & Newman, 1990). Several studies have found that males with anorexia nervosa are infertile secondary to weight loss (e.g., Andersen & Mickalide, 1983) and have lower levels of key endocrine hormones (Beumont, Beardwood, & Russell, 1972; Crisp, Hsu, Chen, & Wheeler, 1982; Lemaire et al., 1983). In particular, anorexia nervosa in males is usually associated with low plasma testosterone as well as low luteinizing hormone (LH) and follicle-stimulating hormone (FSH) (Mehler & Andersen, 1999).

Notably, a number of studies have shown that testosterone levels remain significantly lower than normal even after weight restoration in many patients with anorexia nervosa. According to Herzog, Bradburn, and Newman (1990), a similar process takes place in females who are slow to recover menses after weight restoration. It has been suggested that these women continue abnormal and unhealthy eating behavior regardless of restored body weight, which interferes with their recovery of healthy menstrual functioning.

Patients with anorexia nervosa show significant deficits in cognitive, emotional, and social functioning compared to healthy, same-age peers (Chui et al., 2008). As a partial explanation of these observations, it has been noted that because the brain requires approximately 20 percent of the body's total energy expenditure for optimal functioning, at low weights the body is not able to protect the brain's integrity (Treasure, Wack, & Roberts, 2008). Indeed, anorexia nervosa is associated with significant loss of cerebral gray and white matter, cerebral atrophy, and enlarged ventricles. And while partial restoration of brain tissue does appear to accompany weight restoration (Joos et al., 2011), it does seem that loss of volume in some areas, such as the precuneus region which is associated with distortions in body image, is permanent (Sachdev, Mondraty, Wen, & Gulliford, 2008).

Refeeding syndrome is a metabolic complication that can develop in the early phases of nutritional replenishment with severely malnourished patients (see Mehler & Andersen, 1999 for a good overview of practical guidelines for refeeding patients with anorexia nervosa). If refeeding syndrome is not addressed, serious complications, such as cardiovascular collapse, can occur (Mehler, Birmingham, Crow, & Jahraus, 2010). Because of this, patients who are 30 percent below their ideal body weight should be immediately referred for inpatient hospitalization (Bermudez & Beightol, 2004).

Osteoporosis is a medical condition in which bones become brittle and fragile as a result of low bone mass and deterioration of the microarchitectural structure of bone. This condition increases risk for bone fracture as a direct result of low bone mass. The majority of skeletal bone growth occurs during childhood and adolescence, with peak growth between ages 17 and 22 – a time period that, unfortunately, often corresponds to the onset of anorexia nervosa (Mehler, Birmingham, Crow, & Jahraus, 2010).

Osteoporosis is typically associated with women. In the general population, 80 percent of those affected by osteoporosis are women (National Osteoporosis Foundation, 2009). Indeed, one protective factor against osteoporosis in healthy males is their higher testosterone levels (Scurlock, Timimi, & Robinson, 1997). As a result, although osteoporosis is widely recognized as a risk factor in females with anorexia nervosa, it is often forgotten in males. In fact, because males with anorexia nervosa have significantly lower testosterone levels than their healthy counterparts, they are not provided with the protection against osteoporosis afforded to healthy men and boys. As it turns out, male patients with anorexia nervosa have been shown to have more extensive osteoporosis than their female counterparts (Mehler, Sabel, Watson, & Andersen, 2008).

Pubertal Process

In the exploratory phase of treatment, Roberto often described a memory from his early adolescence, around age 12. He recalled eating a large meal of his favorite childhood food, enchiladas, with his mother and a family friend. Later in the evening, Roberto returned to his room to change clothes before going to play soccer with school friends. To his alarm, he had difficulty buttoning his pants. While this memory contains a number of elements for further exploration and inquiry, it highlights Roberto's alarm about fast weight gain around the time he entered puberty. Indeed, puberty plays an important role in the development of anorexia nervosa in males. In most boys with anorexia nervosa, onset starts just before or after puberty begins (Scott, 1986).

If puberty begins early and happens quickly, boys may become slightly overweight for their age. In fact, some males are slightly overweight, or even obese, before the onset of anorexia nervosa. In contrast to girls who diet because they feel fat in spite of being at "normal" weight, many boys diet because they have been overweight at some point in their lives. Indeed, pre-morbid obesity in males with anorexia nervosa has frequently been mentioned in the literature (Andersen, 1992; Crisp & Toms, 1972). Pre-morbid obesity may make boys the target of teasing, which, in some cases, plays an important role in the onset of many cases of anorexia nervosa. This potential relationship is explored in more detail in Chapter 6: The Culture and Gender Metaframework.

The idea that rapid onset of early puberty is a risk factor for anorexia nervosa is supported by the fact that the disorder is most prevalent in females, who characteristically experience puberty earlier and have rapid growth with a marked increase in body fat relative to muscle, in comparison to boys (Crisp & Burns, 1990). In contrast with girls, fat is a less intimate part of boys' pubertal process. In girls, the development of breasts is followed by an increase in hip size and subcutaneous fat deposits on the buttocks, abdomen, and thighs. Boys, however, undergo a substantial addition of muscle relative to fat. As a result, boys are less likely to become preoccupied with their body fat.

What makes some boys, many of whom develop anorexia nervosa, sensitive to even developmentally normal increases in body fat? One possibility is that gender identity confusion increases their sensitivity to fat development because of its association to feminine shape (Crisp & Burns, 1990). This possibility is discussed in more detail in Chapter 6: The Culture and Gender Metaframework. And of course, puberty is also a period in which sexual development is emphasized. The relationship between sexual development, which is foregrounded by the pubertal process, and anorexia nervosa in males is discussed in Chapter 8: The Psychodynamic Metaframework.

In the following chapter, we explore the role of culture and gender in anorexia nervosa in men and boys. In particular, we consider the importance of social and cultural experience in shaping male body image and highlight the link between body image and anorexia nervosa. In addition, we discuss the prevalence of anorexia nervosa in male athletes as well as in particular professional groups. After mentioning the prevalence of teasing in the clinical population, we move on to a discussion of gender, gender identity confusion, and sexual orientation in men and boys with anorexia nervosa.

Note

1 For a thorough discussion of the medical complications involved in eating disorders, with a chapter that focuses on male problems in particular, see *Eating Disorders: A Guide to Medical Care and Complications* (Mehler & Andersen, 1999).

References

Andersen, A. (2014). A brief history of eating disorders in males. In L. Cohn & R. Lemberg (Eds.), *Current findings on males with eating disorders* (pp. 4–10). New York: Routledge.

Andersen, A. E. (1992). Eating disorders in males. In R. Lemberg (Ed.), *Controlling eating disorders with facts, advice, and resources* (pp. 21–28). Phoenix, AZ: The Oryx Press.

Andersen, A. E. & Mickalide, A. D. (1983). Anorexia nervosa in the male: An underdiagnosed disorder. *Psychosomatics*, 24, 1066–1075.

Bermudez, O. & Beightol, S. (2004). What is refeeding syndrome? *Eating Disorders*, 12(3), 251–256.

Beaumont, P. J. V., Beardwood, C. J., & Russell, G. F. M. (1972). The occurrence of the syndrome of anorexia nervosa in male subjects. *Psychological Medicine*, 2, 216–231.

Beumont, P. J., Beumont, C. C., Touyz, S. W., & Williams, H. (1997). Nutritional counseling and supervised exercise. In D. M. Garner & P. E. Garfinkel (Eds.), *Handbook of treatment for eating disorders* (pp. 178–187). New York: Guilford.

Bulik, C. M., Sullivan, P. F., Tozzi, F., Furberg, H., Lichtenstein, P., & Pedersen, N. L. (2006). Prevalence, heritability, and prospective risk factors for anorexia nervosa. *Archives of General Psychiatry*, 63(3), 305–312.

Chui, H. T., Christensen, B. K., Zipursky, R. B., Richards, B. A., Hanratty, M. K., Kabani, N. J., Mikulis, D. J., & Katzman, D. K. (2008). Cognitive function and brain structure in females with a history of adolescent-onset anorexia nervosa. *Pediatrics*, *122*(2), 426–437.

Crisp, A. H. & Burns, T. (1990). Primary anorexia nervosa in the male and female: A comparison of clinical features and prognosis. In A. E. Andersen (Ed.), *Males with eating disorders* (pp. 77–99). New York: Brunner/Mazel.

Crisp, A. H. & Toms, D. A. (1972). Primary anorexia nervosa or weight phobia in the male: Report on 13 cases. *British Medical Journal*, *1*, 334–338.

Crisp, A. H., Hsu, L. K. G., Chen, C. N., & Wheeler, M. (1982). Reproductive hormone profiles in male anorexia nervosa before, during and after restoration of body weight to normal: A study of twelve patients. *International Journal of Eating Disorders*, *1*(3), 3–9.

Herzog, D. B., Bradburn, I. S., & Newman, K. (1990). Sexuality in males with eating disorders. In A. E. Andersen (Ed.), *Males with eating disorders* (pp. 40–53). New York: Brunner/Mazel.

Joos, A., Hartmann, A., Glauche, V., Perlov, E., Unterbrink, T., Saum, B., ... & Zeeck, A. (2011). Grey matter deficit in long-term recovered anorexia nervosa patients. *European Eating Disorders Review*, *19*(1), 59–63.

Keys, A., Brozek, J., Henschel, A., & Mickelson, O., & Taylor, H. L. (1950). *The biology of human starvation*. Vols. I–II. Minneapolis, MN: University of Minnesota Press.

Lemaire, A., Ardaens, K., Lepretre, J., Racadot, A., Buvat-Herbaut, M., & Buvat, J. (1983). Gonadal hormones in male anorexia nervosa. *International Journal of Eating Disorders*, *2*(4), 135–144.

Mehler, P. S. & Andersen, A. E. (1999). *Eating disorders: A guide to medical care and complications*. Baltimore, MD: JHU Press.

Mehler, P. S., Birmingham, L. C., Crow, S. J., & Jahraus, J. P. (2010). Medical complications of eating disorders. In C. M. Grilo and J. E. Mitchell (Eds.), *The treatment of eating disorders: A clinical handbook*. (pp. 66–80). New York: Guilford Press.

Mehler, P. S., Sabel, A. L., Watson, T., & Andersen, A. E. (2008). High risk of osteoporosis in male patients with eating disorders. *International Journal of Eating Disorders*, *41*(7), 666–672.

Milosevic, A., Brodie, D. A., & Slade, P. D. (1997). Dental erosion, oral hygiene, and nutrition in eating disorders. *International Journal of Eating Disorders*, *21*(2), 195–199.

National Osteoporosis Foundation (2009). Fast facts on osteoporosis. Retrieved May 2, 2009, from http://www.nof.org/osteoporosis/diseasefacts.htm.

Norris, M. L., Apsimon, M., Harrison, M., Obeid, N., Buchholz, A., Henderson, K. A., & Spettigue, W. (2012). An examination of medical and psychological morbidity in adolescent males with eating disorders. *Eating Disorders*, *20*(5), 405–415.

Sachdev, P., Mondraty, N., Wen, W., & Gulliford, K. (2008). Brains of anorexia nervosa patients process self-images differently from non-self-images: an fMRI study. *Neuropsychologia*, *46*(8), 2161–2168.

Scott, D. W. (1986). Anorexia nervosa in the male: A review of the clinical, epidemiological, and biological findings. *International Journal of Eating Disorders*, *5*, 799–819.

Scurlock, H., Timimi, S., & Robinson, P. H. (1997). Case report: Osteoporosis as a complication of chronic anorexia nervosa in a male. *European Eating Disorders Review*, *5*(1), 42–46.

Treasure, J. L., Wack, E. R., & Roberts, M. E. (2008). Models as a high-risk group: The health implications of a size zero culture. *The British Journal of Psychiatry*, *192*(4), 243–244.

Windauer, U., Lennerts, W., Talbot, P., Touyz, S. W., & Beumont, P. J. (1993). How well are "cured" anorexia nervosa patients? An investigation of 16 weight-recovered anorexic patients. *The British Journal of Psychiatry*, *163*(2), 195–200.

Yager, J. & Andersen, A. E. (2005). Anorexia nervosa. *New England Journal of Medicine*, *353*(14), 1481–1488.

6   The Culture and Gender Metaframework

Zack is a 15-year-old boy who is struggling with his sexual identity and with anorexia nervosa. We are well into treatment and Zack has made significant gains in weight restoration and nutritional rehabilitation. With his medical safety temporarily assured, we begin a deeper exploration of the factors that constrain his full recovery and movement toward healthy attitudes and beliefs about food, weight, and shape. In our work together, which mostly takes place without other members of the patient system present, Zack and I explore the meaning of his symptoms and how they were shaped by his experience of culture and gender, ultimately leading to his crippling engagement with restrictive eating.

The metaframework developed in this chapter concerns the meaning, both cognitive and affective, clients attribute to themselves, each other, and their behavior. Meaning is understood as socially constructed, a product of a person's participation in and allegiance to different cultures (Pinsof, 1995). In this view, culture encompasses both beliefs and practices that are linked to a context defining proper behavior and experience. These contexts include, but are not limited to, socioeconomic status, social class, race, ethnicity, sexual orientation, religion, education, and physical circumstances. Yet another context is gender, which points to a person's beliefs about what it means to be a male or female (Pinsof, 1995). Consistent with the model presented in this book, insofar as factors related to culture and gender constrain the patient system's movement toward health, they are a target of intervention by the patient's treatment team.

We begin this chapter by unpacking the concept of body image, highlighting the ways in which our mental representation of the body is shaped by social forces with an eye toward the experience of men and boys. We discuss the prevalence of anorexia nervosa in male athletes as well as in particular professional groups, such as appearance-based jobs, jobs traditionally held by women, and food-related jobs. After highlighting the prevalence of teasing in the clinical population, we move on to a discussion of gender, gender identity confusion, and sexual orientation in men and boys with the disorder.

Body Image

In *The Image and Appearance of the Human Body* (1950), psychoanalyst Paul Schilder began to think about bodily experience from a psychological and sociological point of view. Previous research focused on distortions in body perception caused by brain damage. In contrast, Schilder defined body image as the picture of ourselves we form in our own minds. Building on this thinking, Grogan (2006) defined body image as a person's perceptions, thoughts, and feelings about his or her body. Her definition incorporated three important elements from Schilder's research: (a) body size estimation (perception), (b) evaluation of body attractiveness (thoughts), and (c) emotions associated with body shape and size (feelings).

As Zack and I explore his experience of embodiment, we can see all three of Grogan's (2006) components of body image emerge.

ZACK: I feel like my stomach is a huge balloon. I'm sitting in class, or talking with you in here, and my attention is always on it.

THERAPIST: It feels like your stomach is enormous…

ZACK: And I hate it. I really do. Like we've talked about, when Joe first starting teasing me about being "poochy" … that's when all of this started. And now when I feel my stomach against my waistband, I really hate it.

THERAPIST: There's a part of you that bought into what Joe said, about you being "poochy" and there being something terribly wrong with that.

ZACK: I think almost all of me agrees with him. It looks awful.

In his first statement, Zack describes his perception that his stomach is a "huge balloon." Yet, as I sit across from him, I am struck by the thinness of his waist. While Zack's experience of his stomach may be over-determined – for example, he may be suffering from bloating and intestinal gas, which will need to be evaluated by his physician – he is clearly having difficulty accurately evaluating the size of his own body (component a). As our exploration progresses, Zack elaborates his painful thoughts and feelings (components b and c) about this area of his body.

As this vignette illustrates, body image is subjective. There may be little correlation between one's subjective experience of the body and its appearance to an outside observer. And indeed, men and boys with anorexia nervosa perceive their body size as much larger than it appears to others. In one study, researchers asked male participants to choose, among 100 possible images with 10 different levels of muscularity and 10 levels of fat, (1) his own body, (2) the body he would like to have, (3) the body of an average man his age, and (4) the male body he believed women would like best.

Results showed that the body ideals of males with anorexia nervosa were no different than the body ideals of controls. While body ideals did not differ, males with anorexia nervosa perceived themselves as twice as fat as they actually were, whereas the control group showed no such distortion (Mangweth et al., 2004). As this experiment suggests, and as clinical research validates, we must not only re-educate men and boys about levels of body fat that are reasonable and appropriate; in addition, patient's perceptions of their own bodies require revision through a long, often difficult, process of exploration.

The Influence of Social Experience on Body Image

Body image is intimately intertwined with cultural experience. We can begin to understand their relationship by exploring the notion of objectified body consciousness. This notion incorporates three ideas: (1) body surveillance, (2) the internalization of cultural body standards, and (3) appearance control beliefs. First, body surveillance involves viewing oneself as separate from one's body. In this way, we measure ourselves against a set of standards and try to meet those standards. Second, the internalization of cultural body standards happens when males experience cultural standards as equivalent to their own desires for their bodies. As a result, males find it increasingly difficult to liberate themselves from unrealistic body ideals. Third, appearance control beliefs trick us into thinking that these cultural standards are achievable (McKinley, 2002).

Garfinkel and Garner (1982) was one of the first studies to show that social experience encourages an exceptionally thin body shape model in females with anorexia nervosa. Since that time, this finding has been repeatedly documented (e.g., Dakanalis & Riva, 2013). Furthermore, the prevalence rates of eating disorders in women have mirrored changes in mass media; as the media ideal has become thinner, the prevalence of anorexia and bulimia nervosa has increased (Harrison & Cantor, 1997).

The internalization of a body shape model begins in childhood and peaks during adolescence, when the risk for developing an eating disorder is greatest. In popular culture, male bodies are increasingly presented as muscular and trim (Andersen, Cohn, & Holbrook, 2000). The number of magazines that emphasize men's appearance has increased enormously in the past decade (Boni, 2002). Advertisements increasingly depict men as sexual objects (Kimmel & Tissier-Desbordes, 1999). Even children's action figures have become more muscular (Xie et al., 2006). As these sociocultural changes have taken root, young men have experienced increasing body dissatisfaction (Adams, Turner, & Bucks, 2005). Many researchers have speculated that the increase in body dissatisfaction stems from greater exposure to ideal bodies in popular culture (Pope, Phillips, & Olivardia, 2000). A recent meta-analysis of 15 studies found that exposure to images of ideal male bodies has a small but statistically significant negative effect on young men's body satisfaction (Blond, 2008).

Furthermore, body dissatisfaction creates a vicious cycle by making males more susceptible to the negative effects of media on body image. In one study, participants were presented with one accurate and six distorted photographs of five thin female celebrities. The distorted photographs made the celebrities appear heavier or thinner than they actually were. Participants choose two photographs, one representing the size they thought the celebrity was and the other her ideal size. Body-dissatisfied males and females judged the actual size of female celebrities as thinner than they actually were. With these results in hand, researchers suggested that body-dissatisfied individuals may suffer more negative effects from media than body-satisfied individuals because they perceive media images differently and have different attitudes toward ideal body size (Willinge, Touyz & Charles, 2006).

Athletics

For most of us, sports provides a form of recreation and exercise, a means of managing stress, and an opportunity for bonding with fellow players. Indeed, while involvement in athletics may improve body image, enhance psychological well-being, and even decrease inclination to diet, it has also been noted that participation in sports may be a predisposing factor in the development of eating disorders or a strongly predictive one (Mehler & Andersen, 2010). In particular, it is well-known that female athletes in sports that emphasize slimness for appearance or performance are at a markedly increased risk for developing anorexia nervosa (Mehler & Andersen, 2010).

Men and boys who participate in sports are especially vulnerable to developing anorexia nervosa (Andersen, Cohn, & Holbrook, 2000; Wooldridge & Lytle, 2012). What predisposes male athletes to anorexia nervosa? The most important factor is the nature of the sport that the male athlete participates in, though whether more predisposed men and boys are attracted to certain sports remains in question (Mehler & Andersen, 2010).

Anorexia nervosa is most prevalent in three types of sports with male participants. The first are sports where aesthetics are critical to the scoring process. This includes figure skating, diving, dance, and gymnastics. The second are sports in which the athlete has to "make weight" for competition. Gymnasts, runners, body builders, rowers, wrestlers, jockeys, dancers, and swimmers are especially vulnerable to eating disorders because their sports require weight restriction (Andersen, Bartlett, Morgan, & Brownell, 1995). The third are sports where low body weight is advantageous for performance. Low body weight is correlated with enhanced performance in sports such as track and field, cross-country and other forms of long-distance running, and swimming (Baum, 2006).

One study of male wrestlers and rowers, all competing in low-weight divisions, found an increase in the prevalence of subclinical eating disorders when compared to non-athlete controls (Thiel, Gottfried, & Hesse, 1993). Male jockeys are more susceptible than females since women are naturally lighter and smaller. Many jockeys sit in heated cars wearing rubber suits to lose weight. An article in the *Los Angeles Times* quoted one jockey who said, "for many jockeys, the hot-box is their home away from home." According to this article, 67 percent of jockeys use hot-box saunas (Christine, 2001). Similarly, many crew athletes go on "sweat runs," wearing many layers of clothing while running in hot weather (Baum, 2006).

Elite athletes, in particular, experience tremendous pressure to succeed and to enhance their physical capacities. Particular psychological features that may factor into athletic participation, especially in elite athletics, may also predispose male patients into developing anorexia nervosa. For example, an external locus of control, in which self-esteem is highly dependent upon the approval of others, as well as a sensitivity to rejection will make participation in competitive athletics especially difficult, in addition to making athletes more susceptible to negative feedback or teasing from coaches and peers. Similarly, perfectionism and all-or-nothing thinking may lead to extremes of dieting behavior in order to improve performance (Mehler & Andersen, 2010).

Indeed, competitiveness is an important aspect of anorexia nervosa (Halperin, 1996). While all children experience competition, it has been suggested that, in some cases, parents of children with anorexia nervosa may be poor role models of frustration tolerance and disappointment. Because these children lack a model of how to enjoy competitive situations without winning, they become increasingly driven in their athletic pursuits. Unfortunately, sports that emphasize the body may channel that drive into the pursuit of thinness for better performance (Baum, 2006).

Coaches play an important role in the effect sports have on male participants. Indeed, coaches can either promote eating disorders among athletes or be partners in treatment, promoting full recovery instead of merely a return to sports participation (Mehler & Andersen, 2010). For example, Biesecker and Martz (1999) compared the responses of male and female athletes to negative (emphasis on performance) and positive (emphasis on health) coaching vignettes in relation to body weight. They found that both males and females responded more pathologically to the negative vignette, with more thoughts about dieting, anxiety about body image, and fear of fat. Elsewhere, it has been noted that 67 percent of athletes with eating disorders reported that they were dieting because of their coach's instructions (Sundgot-Borgen, 1994).

Athletic injury may also trigger the development of anorexia nervosa and other eating disorders (Mehler & Andersen, 2010). Many patients invest the entirety of their energies into athletic pursuits and, in the process, fail to develop identities grounded outside of sports. In many cases, their friendships may also be tied up with athletic involvement. When participation in sports becomes unavailable – in many cases, as a result of an injury that makes practice and competition impossible – anxiety is heightened. In addition, athletes may attempt to compensate for their reduced energy expenditure with dieting which, in turn, spirals into significant eating pathology (Mehler & Andersen, 2010).

Professional Interests

Men and boys with anorexia nervosa tend to be in different subsets of the population than females (Garner & Garfinkel, 1980). In one study of 109 males with eating disorders, 17 (16 percent) were in high-risk jobs, including appearance-based jobs (e.g., modeling, acting), jobs traditionally held by women (e.g., floriculture, nursing), and food-related jobs (e.g., catering, restaurant management). In many cases, the job was clearly related to the onset of the eating disorder (Carlat, Camargo, & Herzog, 1997)

Zack often tells me about his aspirations to become an actor. In our explorations, we frequently discuss this fantasy and its appeal for him, as in the following excerpt:

ZACK: I've always imagined myself in Hollywood or New York in a few years. For a while I thought that might not happen because I was so sick. But now I've started to think about it again... it's sort of embarrassing.

THERAPIST: Something draws you to Hollywood or New York.

ZACK: That's where the acting happens. You know that I love theater and if I want to make a go of that, I think that's where I'd have to be. And you know, I admire actors so much – Brad Pitt is beautiful and powerful and engaging...

THERAPIST: In the theater, you'd be up on stage... admired by people around you. I'm thinking about how you haven't felt that way in the past; actually, you've felt criticized by people who were close to you.

ZACK: Yeah. It was humiliating when Joe teased me – especially that time when all my other teammates were watching.

Here, we can see that the idea becoming an actor holds particular appeal for Zack because it offers an attempt to master his prior experiences of humiliation at the hands of a fellow teammate. By imagining himself as an actor, Zack envisions his body as an object of admiration. In addition, Zack's developing sexuality is apparent in his fantasy and raises questions about his sexual orientation – a topic of future conversation.

Teasing

Males with anorexia nervosa often have a history of weight-related teasing (Andersen, Cohn, & Holbrook, 2000). Peer criticism about weight was reported as a precipitant factor in a large number of cases in several studies. These boys were hypersensitive to teasing about "plumpness" or "pudginess" (Sterling & Segal, 1985). Sharp, Clark, Dunan, Blackwood, and Shapiro (1994) found that in a sample of 24 males with anorexia nervosa, 3 recalled being teased about their weight.

This vulnerability to teasing likely dovetails with other factors, such as vulnerable self-esteem and sensitivity to rejection. In my clinical practice, I have repeatedly noted the ways that male patients who struggle with food, weight, and shape have been sensitized to their bodily "imperfections" through experiences of criticism and teasing. Insofar as these experiences continue to motivate dieting behavior and problematic attitudes and beliefs, they are constraints that must be addressed in treatment.

The Role of Gender

Gender refers to socially constructed ideas of masculinity and femininity. In fact, because dieting and concerns about a slim physique are less culturally acceptable for boys and men, they may describe their struggles with anorexia nervosa in different ways than girls and women. While girls and women with anorexia nervosa usually report wanting a "thin" physique, boys and men often describe their compulsive exercise and dieting as a wish to "get strong" or as the pursuit of an athletic build with good muscle definition (Hamlett & Curry, 1990). Yet many men and boys with anorexia nervosa do, in fact, describe their desires for their bodies in typically "feminine" language.

Regardless, men and boys diagnosed with anorexia nervosa are more likely to be thought of by health professionals as feminine and as having an atypical masculine identity (Hepworth, 1999). Indeed, anorexia nervosa is more commonly attributed to males with an inadequately developed masculine gender identity (Romero, 1994). In addition, men account for the diagnosis of anorexia nervosa in men through reference to femininity and mental weakness (McVittie, Cavers, & Hepworth, 2005). Ultimately, it is often extremely difficult for males with anorexia nervosa to come forward for fear that they will be thought of as less masculine (Soban, 2006).

Zack and I spent considerable time thinking about masculinity and femininity and gender identity. Late in the treatment process, the following dialogue occurred:

ZACK: I know that I'm not the most masculine guy – not as it's usually defined. When I look around at school – those idiots on the football team or whatever – I don't compare to that at all. I'm not even interested in those things.

THERAPIST: You're asking an important question about where you fit in…

ZACK: Sometimes I wonder whether I'm a man. I think I am, but then I look around – even at my father, you know? I'm nothing like him.

THERAPIST: And it raises a question about what it means to be a man.

ZACK: Yeah. Is there any place for me in that category?

In this excerpt, we see Zack begin to struggle with sorting out his own gender identity. He is thinking about what it means to be a man and, noting the differences between himself and other men that he has observed, especially his father, struggling to find a place for himself on the gender continuum. As treatment proceeds, we continue to explore these issues and how they may have contributed to his flight from growing up which, for Zack, meant fully embodying his masculine body and sexual identity.

Increased weight in boys almost certainly has fewer sexual implications than in girls, for whom weight increases are associated with the development of a feminine figure or pregnancy (Andersen & Mickalide, 1983). However, the development of body fat may be associated with the feminine shape by many boys with anorexia nervosa (Crisp & Burns, 1990). In fact, this was the case with Zack who is described above.

Researchers have also speculated that there is an association between gender identity confusion and anorexia nervosa in males. Gender identity disorder (GID) is a rare disorder with a prevalence of 1 in 10,000 in males and 1 in 30,000 in females (DSM-IV-TR). There are two reasons to believe that gender identity disorder and anorexia nervosa are related. First, both disorders involve preoccupation with body shape. Second, a large proportion of male patients with anorexia nervosa have evidenced disturbed psychosexual and/or gender identity development (Fitcher & Daser, 1987).

In a recent study of college-aged youth, an eating disorder diagnosis as well as use of diet pills, vomiting, and laxative use were highest among transgender youth compared to heterosexual and homosexual men and women (Diemer, Grant, Munn-Chernoff, Patterson, & Duncan, 2015). In another study of two patients with gender identity disorder and anorexia nervosa, both men wanted to lose weight to achieve a more feminine shape. Furthermore, one of the patients showed marked improvement in body satisfaction and self-esteem after gender reassignment surgery (Winston, Acharya, Chaudhuri, & Fellowes, 2004).

Homosexuality

Homosexuality has been identified as a risk factor for eating disorders in men and boys (Andersen, 1990). While the proportion of male homosexuals in the general population is estimated at 3–5 percent (Whitman, 1983), the percentage of homosexuals in the population of males with eating disorders is likely twice as high (Fichter & Daser, 1987). The most widespread explanation for the increased incidence of anorexia nervosa in the homosexual population is that gay men experience more body dissatisfaction than heterosexual men (Andersen, Cohn, & Holbrook, 2000).

According to one study, gay men were objectively no further away from their body ideals than heterosexual men. In spite of this, gay men experienced significantly more emotional and cognitive bodily dissatisfaction than their heterosexual counterparts. Furthermore, gay men were more psychologically distressed than heterosexual men. Interestingly, most of their psychosocial concerns were roughly equivalent to those reported by women. In gay men and women, self-esteem was significantly impacted by body dissatisfaction (Beren, Hayden, Wilfley, & Grilo, 1999).

Indeed, Herzog, Bradburn, and Newman (1990) suggested that homosexual men experience a cultural pressure to remain thin similar to the pressure experienced by women. However, one exception to this idea is that gay men reported significantly more general and weight-specific teasing than any other group. It is difficult to know whether gay men are teased more as boys or whether they are more sensitive to being teased. Affiliation with the gay community was also a significant predictor of body dissatisfaction in gay men. Men in the gay community reported more pressure to diet in comparison to unaffiliated gay men and heterosexual men.

Researchers have also suggested that gay and bisexual men are at increased risk for eating disorders because of the greater incidence of childhood sexual abuse in this population (Feldman & Meyer, 2007). There is an association between both physical and sexual abuse in childhood and eating disorders in women (Smolak & Murnen, 2002). Hund and Espelage (2006) suggested that eating disorders develop as an attempt to cope with the overwhelming emotions associated with abuse. More recently, the association between childhood abuse and eating disorders has been found in men (Neumark-Sztainer, Story, Hannan, Beuhring, & Resnick, 2000). Several studies have found that homosexual men are more likely to have experienced victimization and abuse during childhood (e.g., Balsam, Rothblum, & Beauchaine, 2005). However, one study suggested that childhood sexual abuse was more highly associated with the symptoms of bulimia, such as binging and purging, than with anorexia nervosa in the homosexual population (Feldman & Meyer, 2007). Other studies have also reported that childhood sexual abuse is more strongly associated with the binge–purge subtype of anorexia nervosa (Carter, Bewell, Blackmore, & Woodside, 2006).

In the following chapter, we continue our exploration of cultural factors implicated in anorexia nervosa. In particular, we discuss the pro-anorexia movement, which takes an at least partially positive attitude toward anorexia nervosa and other eating disorders. The movement, which largely occurs online, is increasingly seen in clinical practice and demands the attention of clinicians and researchers. When patients are involved in these forums, that involvement becomes a constraint on the problem-maintenance space that must be addressed to facilitate the patient system's movement toward health.

References

Adams, G., Turner, H., & Bucks, R. (2005). The experience of body dissatisfaction in men. *Body Image, 2*, 271–283.

Andersen, A. E. (1990). Diagnosis and treatment of males with eating disorders. In A. E. Andersen (Ed.), *Males with eating disorders* (pp. 133–162). New York: Brunner/Mazel, Inc.

Andersen, A. E., Bartlett, S. J., Morgan, G. D., & Brownell, K. D. (1995). Weight loss, psychological, and nutritional patterns in competitive male body builders. *International Journal of Eating Disorders, 18*, 49–57.

Andersen, A. E. & Mickalide, A. D. (1983). Anorexia nervosa in the male: An underdiagnosed disorder. *Psychosomatics, 24*, 1066–1075.

Andersen, A. E., Cohn, L., & Holbrook, T. (2000). *Making weight: Healing men's conflicts with food, weight, and shape.* Carlsbad, CA: Gürze Books.

Balsam, K. F., Rothblum, E. D., & Beauchaine, T. P. (2005). Victimization over the life span: A comparison of lesbian, gay, bisexual, and heterosexual siblings. *Journal of Consulting and Clinical Psychology, 73*(3), 477–487.

Baum, A. (2006). Eating disorders in the male athlete. *Sports Medicine, 36*(1), 1–6.

Beren, S. E., Hayden, H. A., Wilfley, D. E., & Grilo, C. M. (1999). The influence of sexual orientation on body dissatisfaction in adult men and women. *International Journal of Eating Disorders, 20*(2), 135–141.

Biesecker, A. C. & Martz, D. M. (1999). Impact of coaching style on vulnerability for eating disorders: An analog study. *Eating Disorders, 7*(3), 235–244.

Blond, A. (2008). Impact of exposure to images of ideal bodies on male body dissatisfaction: A review. *Body Image, 5*(3), 244–250.

Boni, F. (2002). Framing media masculinities: Men's lifestyle magazines and the biopolitics of the male body. *European Journal of Communication, 17*, 465–478.

Carlat, D. J., Camargo, C. A., & Herzog, D. B. (1997). Eating disorders in males: A report on 135 patients. *American Journal of Psychiatry, 154*(8), 1127–1131.

Carter, J. C. Bewell, C., Blackmore, E., & Woodside, D. B. (2006). The impact of sexual abuse in anorexia nervosa. *Child Abuse & Neglect, 30*(3), 257–269.

Christine, B. (2001, February 3). Body blows: Jockey's never-ending weight battles can have deadly results. *Los Angeles Times*, p. D1.

Crisp, A. H. & Burns, T. (1990). Primary anorexia nervosa in the male and female: A comparison of clinical features and prognosis. In A. E. Andersen (Ed.), *Males with eating disorders* (pp. 77–99). New York: Brunner/Mazel.

Dakanalis, A. & Riva, G. (2013). Current considerations for eating and body-related disorders among men. In L. Sams & J. A. Keels (Eds.), *Handbook on body image: Gender differences, sociocultural influences and health implications* (pp. 195–216). New York: Nova Science Publishers.

Diemer, E. W., Grant, J. D., Munn-Chernoff, M. A., Patterson, D. A., & Duncan, A. E. (2015). Gender identity, sexual orientation, and eating-related pathology in a national sample of college students. *Journal of Adolescent Health, 57*(2),144–149.

Feldman, M. B. & Meyer, I. H. (2007). Childhood abuse and eating disorders in gay and bisexual men. *International Journal of Eating Disorders, 40*(5), 418–423.

Fichter, M. M. & Daser, C. (1987). Symptomatology, psychosexual development, and gender identity in 42 anorexic males. *Psychological Medicine, 17,* 409–418.

Garfinkel, P. E. & Garner, D. M. (1982). *Anorexia nervosa: A multidimensional perspective.* New York: Brunner/Mazel.

Garner, D. M. & Garfinkel, P. E. (1980). Sociocultural factors in the development of anorexia nervosa. *Psychological Medicine, 10,* 647–656.

Grogan, S. (2006). Body image and health contemporary perspectives. *Journal of health psychology, 11*(4), 523–530.

Halperin, E. N. (1996). The role of socialization in male anorexia nervosa: Two cases. *Child Psychiatry and Human Development, 26*(3), 159–168.

Hamlett, K. W. & Curry, J. F. (1990). Anorexia nervosa in adolescent males: A review and case study. *Child Psychiatry and Human Development, 21*(2), 79–94.

Harrison, K. & Cantor, J. (1997). The relationship between media consumption and eating disorders. *Journal of Communication, 47,* 40–67.

Hepworth, J. (1999). *The social construction of anorexia nervosa* (Inquiries in Social Construction series). London: Sage Publications.

Herzog, D. B., Bradburn, I. S., & Newman, K. (1990). Sexuality in males with eating disorders. In A. E. Andersen (Ed.), *Males with eating disorders* (pp. 40–53). New York: Brunner/Mazel.

Hund, A. R. & Espelage, D. L. (2006). Childhood emotional abuse and disordered eating among undergraduate females: Mediating influence of alexithymia and distress. *Child Abuse & Neglect, 30*(4), 393–407.

Kimmel, A. J. & Tissier-Desbordes, E. (1999). Males, masculinity and consumption: An exploratory investigation. *European Advances in Consumer Research, 4,* 243–251.

Mangweth, B., Hausmann, A., Walch, T., Hotter, A., Rupp, C. I., Biebl, W., ... Pope Jr., H. G. (2004). Body fat perception in eating-disordered men. *International Journal of Eating Disorders, 35,* 102–108.

McKinley, N. (2002). *Feminist perspectives and objectified body consciousness.* In T. Cash & T. Pruzinsky (Eds.), *Body image: A handbook of theory, research, and clinical practice* (pp. 55–64). New York: The Guilford Press.

McVittie, C., Cavers, D., & Hepworth, J. (2005). Femininity, mental weakness, and difference: Male students account for anorexia nervosa in men. *Sex Roles, 53*(5–6), 413–418.

Mehler, P. S. & Andersen, A. E. (2010). *Eating disorders: A guide to medical care and complications.* Baltimore, MD: JHU Press.

Neumark-Sztainer, D., Story, M., Hannan, P. J., Beuhring, T., & Resnick, M. D. (2000). Disordered eating among adolescents: Associations with sexual/physical abuse and other familial/psychosocial factors. *International Journal of Eating Disorders, 28*(3), 249–258.

Pinsof, W. M. (1995). *Integrative problem-centered therapy: A synthesis of family, individual, and biological therapies.* New York: Basic Books.

Pope, H. G., Phillips, K. A., & Olivardia, R. (2000). *The Adonis complex: How to identify, treat, and prevent body obsession in men and boys.* New York: Touchstone.

Romero, F. (1994). Adolescent boys and anorexia nervosa. *Adolescence*, 29(115), 643–647.

Schilder, P. (1950). *The image and appearance of the human body: Studies in the constructive energies of the psyche.* New York: International Universities Press, Inc.

Sharp, C. W., Clark, S. A., Dunan, J. R., Blackwood, D. H., & Shapiro, C. M. (1994). Clinical presentation of anorexia nervosa in males: 24 new cases. *International Journal of Eating Disorders*, 15(2), 125–134.

Smolak, L. & Murnen, S. K. (2002). A meta-analytic examination of the relationship between child sexual abuse and eating disorders. *International Journal of Eating Disorders*, 31(2), 136–150.

Soban, C. (2006). What about the boys?: Addressing issues of masculinity within male anorexia nervosa in a feminist therapeutic environment. *International Journal of Men's Health*, 5(3), 251–267.

Sterling, J. W. & Segal, J. D. (1985). Anorexia nervosa in males: A critical review. *International Journal of Eating Disorders*, 4(4), 559–572.

Sundgot-Borgen, J. (1994). Risk and trigger factors for the development of eating disorders in female elite athletes. *Medicine & Science in Sports & Exercise*, 26(4), 414–419.

Thiel, A., Gottfried, H., & Hesse, F. W. (1993). Subclinical eating disorders in male athletes. *Acta Psychiatrica Scandinavica*, 88(4), 259–265.

Whitman, F. L. (1983). Culturally invariable properties of male homosexuality: Tentative conclusions from cross-cultural research. *Archives of Sexual Behavior*, 12, 207–226.

Willinge, A., Touyz, S., & Charles, M. (2006). How do body-dissatisfied and body-satisfied males and females judge the size of thin female celebrities? *International Journal of Eating Disorders*, 39(7), 576–582.

Winston, A. P., Acharya, S., Chaudhuri, S., & Fellowes, L. (2004). Anorexia nervosa and gender identity disorder in biologic males: A report of two cases. *International Journal of Eating Disorders*, 36(1), 109–113.

Wooldridge, T. & Lytle, P. (2012). An overview of anorexia nervosa in males. *Eating Disorders: Journal of Treatment & Prevention*, 20(5), 368–378.

Xie, B., Chou, C. P., Spruijt-Metz, D., Reynolds, K., Clark, F., Palmer, P. H., … Johnson, C. A. (2006). Weight perception and weight-related sociocultural and behavioral factors in Chinese adolescents. *Preventive Medicine*, 42, 229–234.

7   Expanding into Cyberspace

Over the past 15 years, a cultural phenomenon termed "pro-anorexia" or "pro-ana" has raised intense controversy. Taking an at least partially positive attitude toward anorexia nervosa and other eating disorders, this movement largely takes place on the Internet in the form of websites, with content ranging from discussion forums, guidelines for beginning and maintaining anorexia, tips for rapid weight loss, dieting competitions, ways to avoid detection by family and friends, and motivational images (e.g., "thinspiration") to inspire further weight loss (Strife & Rickard, 2011).

Because of their increasing popularity, pro-anorexia forums often appear in the indirect patient system – indeed, patient's interactions with other members of the forums need to be understood and addressed in treatment. In addition, these forums create constraints that need to be addressed for successful resolution of the presenting problem. Because pro-anorexia forums are unfamiliar to many clinicians, I will first provide an overview of the content found on pro-ana sites, drawn largely from my own research (Wooldridge, Mok, & Chiu, 2014). Then I will briefly present a psychoanalytic approach to conceptualizing pro-anorexia forums (Wooldridge, 2014).

It's hard to describe the startling, visceral experience of visiting a pro-ana website for the first time. You're immediately confronted with diatribes against medical and mental health treatments, accompanied by photos of emaciated adolescents that convey a strange combination of starvation and sexuality. In a universe of part objects, participants share their particular obsessions: the space between the thighs, protruding ribcages, hipbones like boomerangs. Upon further investigation, you'll find disquieting discussion about how to improve and maintain eating disorders. How do you throw up without choking on your own vomit? How to "water load" so your doctor won't know you've lost weight? How to curb the insistence of the body's appetite?

Like anorexia nervosa itself, pro-ana sites confront visitors with what has been described as "the spectacle of not eating" – words and images conveying profound degrees of emaciation and embodied images of suffering (Warin, 2004). But to the surprise of the media and the medical community, which has almost uniformly condemned pro-ana sites, there's more to the story. As you continue to read, you'll find that participants are making real attempts at connection. "You're a good person," they say to each other, "and we want to support you whether you get worse, stay the same, or eventually recover." And there's a palpable sense of appreciation in the community. Participants speak of their loneliness and how, on these sites, they've found true peers for the first time.

The pro-ana community does not reflect a single philosophy. In addition, participants on pro-ana sites span a variety of diagnostic and demographic groups and further research in this area is sorely needed. Each site has its own unique perspective of what it means to have an eating disorder – for example, whether eating disorders are a lifestyle or a medical condition (Strife & Rickard, 2011), a positive or negative experience (or both). According to some, pro-ana sites serve as a coping mechanism for the emotional pain of eating disorders (Mulveen & Hepworth, 2006). From another perspective, pro-ana participants seek sympathy from like-minded peers, as eating disorders are viewed as "irrational and self-inflicted" by outsiders (Rich, 2006, p. 301).

The pro-ana movement has raised concern among health professionals and parents, who express alarm that these forums may harm vulnerable individuals (Paquette, 2002). Estimates suggest that more than 500 of these websites exist at a given time, although this number is somewhat unreliable as sites are frequently shut down by their hosts and reopened at new locations (Bardone-Cone & Cass, 2007). Notably, this number vastly exceeds that of recovery-oriented forums (Chesley, Alberts, Klein, & Kreipe, 2003). While it is uncertain how widely these sites are used, one study suggests those who use the sites tend to visit them several times daily (Csipke & Horne, 2007).

The impact of pro-ana forums on participants has been hotly debated. The deleterious effects of pro-ana participation, including decreased self-esteem, appearance self-efficacy, and perceived attractiveness, as well as increased negative affect and perception of being overweight, have been documented (Bardone-Cone & Cass, 2007). In another study, 69.2 percent of patients who used pro-ana sites reported using a new weight loss or purging technique and also reported longer durations of illness and less time in school as a result of health issues (Wilson, Peebles, Hardy, & Litt, 2006).

Recent research has taken a more nuanced point of view, suggesting that pro-ana participation has benefits, including social support, a way to cope with a stigmatized illness, and a means of self-expression (Yeshua-Katz & Martins, 2013). Another study suggested that participants who sought emotional support on pro-ana forums experienced benefit, whereas those who use the sites for sustaining an eating disorder without seeking emotional support were more likely to be harmed (Csipke & Horne, 2007).

Online Behavior

One of the primary benefits derived from pro-ana participation is social support (Mulveen & Hepworth, 2006; Yeshua-Katz & Martins, 2013). Unsurprisingly, social support has numerous potential benefits. It may alleviate loneliness (Joinson, 2003), provide physical and mental health benefits (Stone & Pennebaker, 2002), and offer information and solutions to a wide range of problems (Joinson, 2003).

However, the stigma that individuals with eating disorders, and males with eating disorders in particular, confront makes social support difficult to access in day-to-day life (Yeshua-Katz & Martins, 2013). Indeed, men with anorexia nervosa face the additional stigma of seeking help for a "female problem" (Andersen, Cohn, & Holbrook, 2000). On the Internet, in contrast, it is possible to seek social support among a community of sympathetic others while maintaining anonymity and thus a relative sense of personal safety (Davidson, Pennebaker, & Dickerson, 2000).

In my research, seeking support was the most common activity for males on pro-ana websites. Past research suggests that support is provided in two distinct and contradictory ways: support for further weight loss and support for healthy eating and recovery from eating disorders (Mulveen & Hepworth, 2006). For example, the following participant is seeking support in his efforts toward recovery.

> looking to attempt recovery again, and I'm feeling really passionate about succeeding this time. I'm so done with this chapter of my life, I don't want to restrict and b/p [binge and purge] my brains out all the time. One of the things I've failed to do in the past when attempting recovery is reach out to others doing the same, so I was hoping to find some others on this site who are in whatever stage of recovering just as someone to lean on or even to help encourage. Also, any recovery resources you guys would like to link me to would be great. I need all the help I can get!

While thoughts of recovery were consistently received with understanding and acceptance, recovery isn't discussed very often. In addition to these two types of support seeking, in many cases male participants seek support specifically for their concerns about being a male with an eating disorder (ibid.).

> I'm sick of people labeling me "feminine" and "wannabe" just because I am a guy with an eating disorder-even on these support forums ! I don't mean to say that girls are different from boys when it comes to having an ED, my point is that gender really doesn't have a big effect on who can have an eating disorder, in my opinion . True, more females are diagnosed, but there is so much pressure in society for us

males to be fit, slim and good looking. It just sucks, you know ? I'm tired of my issues being dismissed so much. Sorry for the rant, does anyone have any input for me?

A single request for support is typically met with several responses. In most cases, support is offered when participants fail in their efforts at diet restriction or weight loss, as in the following: "You aren't pathetic. We all make mistakes and sometimes it takes a while to get back on track. You always drop your gains so quick though! This rut won't last forever."

In other cases, the support took the form of actually encouraging participants to protect their physical and psychological health to a greater degree. For example,

> I know its [sic] not easy to take advice when you have an ED [eating disorder] but if you can dude, try to get you [sic] cals [calories] up a little, whatever your [sic] comfortable with. The farther [sic] down in this shit you go the harder it is to get out...

As other research suggests, support is consistently forthcoming regardless of whether participants hope to lose weight or gain weight, begin recovery or end it (Yeshua-Katz & Martins, 2013). Finally, males are particularly likely to offer support to other males struggling with feelings of alienation as men with eating disorders. In response to the question, "As a guy with an ED, am I alone here?" a participant wrote: "You're definitely not alone. I'm on here quite often and I see a few dudes scattered here and there. We gotta [sic] stick together!"

Throughout these communities, there is an ongoing sense that many participants appreciate the social support and venue for self-expression provided. There are numerous instances of community appreciation. In many cases, participants express appreciation for finding a place where they could talk with other males who were struggling with eating disorders, in contrast to the experience of loneliness that marks their day-to-day lives.

> It was incredibly difficult for me to go through high school trying to hide an ED. By not eating it even attracted more attention than if a girl would not have. Now, whenever I tell someone close to me about my eating habits I get crucified and told "oh no, only girls have eating disorders" followed by a long list of discrimination. [This site] is a safe haven for all people, regardless of anything, a place without bias and a place where we are free to be our selves. no one is a minority, we are all people. If I hadn't found this site I don't know if I would have gotten out of high school alive.

The paradox of pro-ana is that sites simultaneously encourage healthy self-expression and provide a sense of belonging and understanding while simultaneously providing encouragement to pursue self-destructive practices. The search for a like-minded community appears to be the most prominent force driving pro-ana forums.

At the same time, participants frequently use pro-ana forums to gain practical information and motivation about weight loss and to provide that information to other users. Practical information includes providing, seeking, or discussing tips and techniques, such as calorie restriction and fasting, for weight loss. Most troubling, in other research, users often report trying out new negative behaviors learned on pro-ana forums in real life (Ransom, La Guardia, Woody, & Boyd, 2010). For example, in the following excerpt a participant answers another's request for ways to reduce hunger.

> Tea is calorie free, as stated before. If you like it sweet, I generally stick with no/low-cal sweeteners. I'm pretty boring in my tea selections. I have green tea and English Breakfast. And Earl Grey is to die for with a little almond milk (1/4 cup is 15 calories).

Another commonly discussed item is thinspiration. In its most common form, "thinspiration" or "thinspo" consists of motivational images of models, actresses and actors, or even site participants, many of which have been modified to make them appear even more emaciated. Other forms of thinspiration include mantras such as, "The best way to maintain the loss is lose even more." Participants frequently requested motivational images of males, stating that it is more difficult to find images of males than females.

> I have trouble finding good male thinspo. What does size zero on a guy look like? Any pics [pictures], cause the link ain't working? I wanna [sic] see what size zero is, and if I'm gonna [sic] strive for it

At other times, participants discuss posted images and develop "favorite" models as sources of thinspiration. In these cases, the image seems to serve as a concrete representation of a yearning for a particular kind of psychological state, as illustrated in the following excerpt: "Have you seen the Machinist? I want to look like Bale. he's got no excess at all, totally ripped. If I could look like that, I think id [sic] be happy with my life for good – ahhhh contentment."

Csipke and Horne (2007) have suggested that participants on pro-ana websites can be divided into two categories: (1) those that actively participate on discussion forums, seeking emotional support from other participants, and (2) participants who fail to make meaningful connections on pro-ana sites. Based on my observations, this appears to be correct. Furthermore, it seems reasonable to think that the first category of user has the potential to experience both benefit and harm, whereas the latter group is exposed to the more damaging features of pro-ana sites without the counterbalance of the social support these forums might provide.

Personal Experience

Unsurprisingly, participants often report craving food, as well as a wide variety of negative feelings. Upon closer analysis, negative affect was expressed about themes ranging from appearance self-evaluations to friendships to health concerns. And as the literature on anorexia nervosa in males would predict (Wooldridge & Lytle, 2012), site participants often report a diminished sex drive.

They often speak of their own alienation. Alienation is an experience of existential estrangement, and loneliness is its affective component (Burton, 1961). Close social relationships suffer as a result of an eating disorder (Tiller et al., 1997). Indeed, online forums serve, in part, to counterbalance the lack of social support received in offline relationships (Ransom, La Guardia, Woody, & Boyd, 2010).

Feelings of loneliness and isolation are reported by many individuals with eating disorders (Levine, 2012) and, in some cases, these feelings are reported to have been problematic before onset (Troop & Bifulco, 2002). Naturally, the experience of loneliness is likely more intense in many males with eating disorders, who feel that they are alone in suffering from a "female problem" (Wooldridge & Lytle, 2012). Loneliness is commonly reported, both in daily life and in pro-ana forums themselves, where the number of female participants vastly outweighs male participants.

> I'm shy posting on sites like this because it is mostly girls. I have nothing against girls but there seems to be a certain antagonistic feeling towards males, it often is. Really I'm just lonely here and everywhere else too.

Males with anorexia nervosa are likely to have had a number of alienating experiences while growing up (Wooldridge & Lytle, 2012). For example, males with anorexia often have a history of weight-related teasing (Andersen, Cohn, & Holbrook, 2000). Perhaps due to the fact that they are often slightly pre-morbidly overweight, these boys may be hypersensitive to teasing about "plumpness" or "pudginess" (Sterling & Segal, 1985).

I believe that the prominence of the experience of alienation explains, in part, the appeal of pro-ana forums. Finding themselves the object of public scrutiny and clinical diagnosis, individuals with anorexia struggle to reconcile their own experiences of anorexia as an empowering state of distinction with symbolic power, with the one-sided representation of anorexia by the media and medical professionals (Warin, 2004).

The experience of anorexia nervosa is fraught with ambivalence (Williams & Reid, 2010). Ambivalence is defined as having both positive and negative feelings, or conflicting motivations, about something. In contrast to most mental health problems, anorexia is seen as positive, at least in part, by patients (Garner & Bemis, 1982). Participants report feeling uncertain about whether anorexia is a "friend" or an "enemy" and whether it is a problem that needs treatment (Colton & Pistrang, 2004), often spending a great deal of time weighing its advantages and disadvantages (Cockell, Geller, & Linden, 2003). Similarly, participants may experience anorexia as an empowering mark of distinction while, at the same time, recognizing that it causes severe damage to their health and well-being (Warin, 2004). In the words of one participant,

> I can't bring myself to be healthy. Why? I'm just not happy. I need some kind of control and I need to feel like I can choose to make the decision NOT to overeat. I have this fear that if I eat normally... I will become fat.

Participants report that anorexia gives them a profound sense of control yet, at the same time, exerts tremendous control over their lives. Naturally, they worry that treatment will deprive them of this control (Reid, Burr, Williams & Hammersley, 2008). Frequently, participants debate whether anorexia is a useful, satisfying tool that should be maintained or whether it is a disease that should be treated (Williams & Reid, 2010).

Both parents and the medical community avoid grappling with the ambivalence inherent in the anorexia by focusing exclusively on weight restoration. Weight is used as the primary indicator of a patient's degree of illness and is the primary focus of treatment (Darcy et al., 2010). Well-intentioned comments from friends and family often focus on weight, ignoring the social and emotional dimensions of the disorder (Rich, 2006).

Not only are resistance to gaining weight and denial of the severity of the disorder central aspects of anorexia (American Psychiatric Association, 2000), patients also report feeling deeply alienated by this approach to treatment. Mukai (1989), for example, describes how anorexia is cast in a starkly negative light by clinicians who quickly seek weight restoration. As a result, patients attempt to resist recovery by seeking alternative ways to maintain an anorexic identity (Rich, 2006). One place patients with anorexia can express their desire to persist in eating-disordered behavior is on pro-anorexia forums (Williams & Reid, 2010).

> Looking at the numbers, the male body is allowed to have less percentage fat than the female body, and we need more calories daily due to muscle mass, so my question is this: doesn't this make an ED really serious for a guy to have? I mean, I've been living on less than 700 calories a day for weeks now and still feel fine, but it scares me

to think this could get really, really bad for me. I do feel something in me pushing to get down to single digits in fat percent now... I don't want this to progress any further. but I just don't want to eat anymore either....

Conceptualizing Pro-Anorexia Forums

I've come to believe that pro-ana forums provide participants with the opportunity to make use of potential space (Winnicott, 1971) for creative play with multiple dimensions of their experience. At the same time, pro-ana forums provide a venue for psychic retreat (Steiner, 1993), an escape from truth and relatedness. Indeed, whether the forum functions as potential space or psychic retreat may vary at each moment in treatment. Because the literature has consistently focused on the harmful impact of pro-ana forums, my formulation highlights the ways that I have been able to generatively leverage patients' usage of them during treatment. Pro-ana forums provide opportunities for creativity and relatedness *in some patients and to some degree.*

Nonetheless, pro-ana forums are intensely disturbing and problematic. Whether we are able to help patients to disengage from these forums at any particular point in treatment through more active interventions – for example, by suggesting recovery-oriented reading materials or by discussing the risks of pro-ana participation or by pro-actively engaging the parental subsystem – is a complicated question and dependent upon the state of the patient system. In the most difficult cases, in my experience there are often periods where this is simply not possible for a multitude of reasons. With this in mind, I ask: Can we relate to the patient's preoccupation while holding in mind that it is, at best, both beneficial *and* harmful and with the hope that healthier avenues toward recovery will become accessible over time?

The architecture of pro-ana forums facilitates the generation of both potential space and psychic retreat. Potential space depends on the capacity to maintain a dialectical process between oneness and separateness, fantasy and reality (Ogden, 1985). For this dialectic to be maintained, the participant has to find ways to manage reality as it presents itself. The high level of control afforded to users of Internet-based forums facilitates the management of disturbing aspects of reality, allowing this dialectical process to be maintained and potential space to be accessed.

At times on pro-anorexia forums, participants seem able to think about the disorder in new ways. In the following example, a participant is beginning to think about recovery in all its dimensions, including weight restoration.

so what's it like exactly to feel normal weight? I gain a pound and feel fat as all hell so I cant [sic] imagine what itd [sic] be like to be looking like people I see walking around. but then I look at em [sic] and they look happy sometimes, it makes me wonder if its [sic] worth it... [anorexia]

In other situations, participants make express appreciation for relational connection and support. As one young man wrote,

Part of why this is the best support site is that people on here are in all stages of [eating] disorders and can come here no matter what they feel about their EDs. I have made real friends here, more than in my RL [real life], where it's so hard.

Pro-ana forums also present participants with the possibility of retreating from the pain inherent in the experience of alienation. Of course, psychic retreats can serve as both pathological organizations or as temporary, self-regulatory private spaces that foster resilience and reconsolidation (Steiner, 1993). The problem, in other words, is not the retreat itself but how the retreat is used. When we emerge from retreat, are we more equipped to deal with the exigencies of day-to-day living? As one participant wrote,

When I come on here and talk, I can actually cope, can get through the rest of the day. This place has given me so much strength. Its [sic] given me the support I need to get treatment, to reach out to friends.

In this excerpt, a participant makes use of a pro-ana forum as a temporary retreat that allows him to refuel, emerging again into the world of relationships less battered and more resilient than before. Others, however, use pro-ana forums as extended retreats; in the words of one participant, "Why bother with people? They'll fuck you up and disappoint you. Better to stay on the computer." Thus, pro-ana forums can become a way to almost entirely avoid relational contact that feels too threatening. As Faber (1984) has written,

[The computer] offers itself to its manipulator as a powerful little world, a powerful little universe, a kind of microcosm, that can be totally mastered, totally controlled, in such a way as to offset, at the unconscious level, early narcissistic wounds experienced in the failure to master, to control, the primary caregiver or "object" (p. 267).

At their worst, pro-ana forums serve as a purely projective container into which participants evacuate their emotional lives in order to dissociate from them.

As I have written this chapter, I have struggled with the same conflicts inherent in the pro-ana movement. Essentially, pro-ana forums attempt to provide a protected space, in which individuals are accepted without judgment. Consider, for example, the following mission statement of one pro-ana forum:

> Imagine you have something within you; something that you think about often; something that consumes such a great part of your life that the general public deems it a disorder because it is something so engrained in you. Imagine having no one to talk to about it. ... [This] is a place for people who "think a certain way" about their bodies and lives to meet and to talk. About anorexia, about family, about relationships, about anything at all. To talk openly, in the hope that they won't be judged, and in the hope that they will be understood.

In many ways, I, too, have wanted to refrain from judgment. In light of the intense reactions pro-anorexia forums provoke in family, friends, and treatment providers, I have attempted to understand their potential risks and benefits. Nonetheless, pro-ana forums remain intensely disturbing. In any treatment, it is hoped that the treatment team can help the patient, over time, to begin disengaging from pro-anorexia forums and eventually to relinquish them entirely. With ongoing emotional support, it is hoped the patient will increasingly make forays into the embodied relational world that surrounds him.

References

American Psychiatric Association. (2000). *Diagnostic and statistical manual of mental disorders* (4th ed., text rev.). Washington, DC: Author.

Andersen, A., Cohn, L., & Holbrook, T. (2000). *Making weight: Men's conflicts with food, weight, shape, & appearance.* Carlsbad, CA: Gurze Books.

Bardone-Cone, A. M. & Cass, K. M. (2007). What does viewing a pro-anorexia website do? An experimental examination of website exposure and moderating effects. *The International Journal of Eating Disorders, 40*(6), 537–548.

Burton, A. (1961). On the nature of loneliness. *American Journal of Psychoanalysis, 21,* 34–39.

Chesley, E. B., Alberts, J. D., Klein, J. D., & Kreipe, R. E. (2003). Pro or con? Anorexia nervosa and the Internet. *Journal of Adolescent Health, 32*(2), 123–124.

Cockell, S. J., Geller, J., & Linden, W. (2003). Decisional balance in anorexia nervosa: Capitalizing on ambivalence. *European Eating Disorders Review, 11*(2), 75–89.

Colton, A. & Pistrang, N. (2004). Adolescents' experiences of inpatient treatment for anorexia nervosa. *European Eating Disorders Review, 12*(5), 307–316.

Csipke, E. & Horne, O. (2007). Pro-eating disorder websites: User's opinions. *European Eating Disorders Review, 15*(3), 196–206.

Darcy, A. M., Katz, S., Fitzpatrick, K. K., Forsberg, S., Utzinger, L., & Lock, J. (2010). All better? How former anorexia nervosa patients define recovery and engaged in treatment. *European Eating Disorders Review, 18*(4), 260–270.

Davidson, K. P., Pennebaker, J. W., & Dickerson, S. S. (2000). Who talks? The social psychology of illness support groups. *American Psychologist, 55*, 205–217.

Faber, M. D. (1984). The computer, the technological order, and psychoanalysis: Preliminary remarks. *Psychoanalytic Review, 71*(2), 263–277.

Garner, D. M. & Bemis, K. M. (1982). A cognitive-behavioral approach to anorexia nervosa. *Cognitive Therapy and Research, 6*(2), 123–150.

Joinson, A. N. (2003). *Understanding the psychology of Internet behaviour: Virtual worlds, real lives.* New York: Palgrave Macmillan.

Levine, M. P. (2012). Loneliness and eating disorders. *The Journal of Psychology, 146*(1–2), 243–257.

Mukai, T. (1989). A call for our language: Anorexia from within. *Women's Studies International Forum, 12*(6), 613–638.

Mulveen, R. & Hepworth, J. (2006). An interpretative phenomenological analysis of participation in pro-anorexia sites and its relationship with disordered eating. *Journal of Health Psychology, 11*(2), 283–296.

Ogden, T. (1985). On potential space. *The International Journal of Psychoanalysis, 66*, 129–141.

Paquette, M. (2002). Bad company: Internet sites with dangerous information. *Perspectives in Psychiatric Care, 38*(2), 39–40.

Ransom, D. C., La Guardia, J. G., Woody, E. Z., & Boyd, J. L. (2010). Interpersonal interactions on online forums addressing eating concerns. *International Journal of Eating Disorders, 43*(2), 161–170.

Reid, M., Burr, J., Williams, S., & Hammersley, R. (2008). Eating disorders patients' views on their disorders and on an outpatient service: A qualitative study. *Journal of Health Psychology, 13*(7), 956–960.

Rich, E. (2006). Anorexic dis(connection): Managing anorexia as an illness and an identity. *Sociology of Health & Illness, 28*(30), 284–305.

Steiner, J. (1993). *Psychic retreats: Pathological organizations in psychotic, neurotic, and borderline patients.* New York: Routledge.

Sterling, J. W. & Segal, J. D. (1985). Anorexia nervosa in males: A critical review. *International Journal of Eating Disorders, 4*(4), 559–572.

Stone, L. D. & Pennebaker, J. W. (2002). Trauma in real time: Talking and avoiding online conversations about the death of Princess Diana. *Basic and Applied Social Psychology, 24*, 172–182.

Strife, R. S. & Rickard, K. (2011). The conceptualization of anorexia: The pro-ana perspective. *Journal of Women and Social Work, 26*(2), 213–217.

Tiller, J. M., Sloane, G., Schmidt, U., Troop, N., Power, M., & Treasure, J. L. (1997). Social support in patients with anorexia nervosa and bulimia nervosa. *International Journal of Eating Disorders, 21*(1), 31–38.

Troop, N. A. & Bifulco, A. (2002). Childhood social arena and cognitive sets in eating disorders. *The British Journal of Clinical Psychology, 41*(2), 205–211.

Warin, M. (2004). Primitivising anorexia: The irresistible spectacle of not eating. *The Australian Journal of Anthropology, 15*(1), 95–104.

Williams, S. & Reid, M. (2010). Understanding the experience of ambivalence in anorexia nervosa: The maintainer's perspective. *Psychology & Health, 25*(5), 551–567.

Wilson, J. L., Peebles, R., Hardy, K. K., & Litt, I. F. (2006). Surfing for thinness: A pilot study of pro-eating disorder web site usage in adolescents with eating disorders. *Pediatrics, 118*, 1635–1643.

Winnicott, D. W. (1971). *Playing and reality.* New York: Basic Books.

Wooldridge, T. (2014). The enigma of ana: A psychoanalytic exploration of pro-ana forums. *The Journal of Infant, Child, and Adolescent Psychotherapy, 13*(2), 202–216.

Wooldridge, T. & Lytle, P. (2012). An overview of anorexia nervosa in males. *Eating Disorders: Journal of Treatment & Prevention, 20*(5), 368–378.

Wooldridge, T., Mok, C., & Chiu, S. (2014). A qualitative content analysis of male participation in pro-anorexia forums. *Eating Disorders: Journal of Treatment and Prevention, 22*(2), 97–110.

Yeshua-Katz, D. & Martins, N. (2013). Communicating stigma: The pro-ana paradox. *Health Communications, 28*(5), 499–508.

8 The Psychodynamic Metaframework

Sam is a 15-year-old male with anorexia nervosa who was referred to me for individual therapy by a clinician working with the family as a whole. In our first meeting, I am struck by his height – he stands nearly 6' 2" tall – and by the prominent muscles in his arms. As I later learn, Sam is avidly interested in body building and, before treatment, often spent several hours at the gym each day. After sustaining a shoulder injury that made upper body exercise impossible, Sam began to limit his diet to high protein foods and, over several months, his eating became increasingly restricted.

Sam has been working with a nutritionist and family therapist for three months and has made significant progress in restoring normal eating patterns. The family therapist is concerned, however, by Sam's unremitting low self-esteem and depression. In addition, Sam's mother struggles with severe anxiety and depression and the family therapist worries about the impact of this on Sam. In our first meeting, Sam and I agree to begin a process of twice-weekly psychodynamic psychotherapy to explore these concerns.

The psychodynamic metaframework recognizes that anorexia nervosa may manifest as a result of vastly different intrapsychic factors. Indeed, symptoms may appear in a relatively intact and structured psyche as a reflection of an internal conflict or, on the other end of the continuum, in a psyche with a much less developed mental structure. In this chapter, we outline three possibilities. First, symptoms of anorexia nervosa may be symbolic expressions of psychic aims or defenses, which is encompassed in the drive-conflict model. Second, symptoms may be symbolic expressions of distorted self and object representations, as captured in the object relations model. And third, symptoms may be nonsymbolic emergency measures to manage disrupted self-states threatened with the loss of the self's cohesion, as described by the self-psychological model (Goodsitt, 1997). In clinical practice we typically encounter a combination of these three possibilities. After outlining these three separate but intertwined ways of thinking about anorexia nervosa, we conclude with thoughts about the relationship between the development of the disorder and male psychosexual development.

Drive-Conflict Model

The drive-conflict model was articulated by Freud (1923/1961). Situated in late nineteenth and early 20th century Vienna, Freud's patients lived in a highly structured and sexually oppressive society. In line with this, his patients presented with intense sexual conflict and the drive-conflict model was applicable to these problems, providing a way for him to think about how restrictive societal prohibitions were internalized and in conflict with uncivilized, instinctual forces always pressing for expression (Goodsitt, 1997).

According to the drive-conflict model, psychopathology results from internal conflict between three mental agencies: id, ego, and superego. In this tripartite model, Freud assumed that the psyche already possesses distinct structure. The id, understood to be a cauldron of instinctual drives, constantly presses for expression and operates according to the pleasure principle, seeking to gratify its wishes regardless of their consequences. The superego, in contrast, has incorporated the values and morals of the larger culture. The ego, operating according to the reality principles, attempts to mediate between the id and superego while accounting for the importance of external reality (Freud, 1923/1961).

In this model, symptoms represent symbolic expressions of sexual and aggressive aims as well as defenses against these aims. Thinking in this way, a number of early clinicians linked anorexia nervosa and other eating disorders to problems in the oral phase of psychosexual development, highlighting the massively punitive superego and extreme denial that accompanied patients' normal oral impulses. In addition, a number of early clinicians suggested that self-starvation was a defense against fantasies of oral impregnation (Waller, Kaufman, & Deutsch, 1940; Moulton, 1942; Rowland, 1970). Naturally, this excluded male patients from diagnosis with anorexia nervosa. Still other clinicians saw the patient's refusal of food as a defense against oral sadistic fantasies (Masserman, 1941; Berlin, Boatman, Scheimo, & Szurek, 1951). While these particular formulations are cited less often in today's research and practice, the tripartite model provides clinicians with a way of thinking about the symbolic meaning of symptoms as well as patients' ongoing efforts to negotiate a balance between these three aspects of the self, which are often at cross purposes.

In Sam's treatment, we frequently discuss the harsh and unforgiving "inner critic," or superego, that accompanies him through day-to-day life. Indeed, Sam often tells me about the "horrible names" that he calls himself when he eats something with sugar and fat. In the early stages of treatment, Sam's harsh and unyielding superego was largely unconscious. Over time, we have increasingly articulated its voice and are beginning to talk about what it might be protecting him from, as illustrated in the following excerpt:

SAM: Every time I feel full that voice we've been talking about starts. Fat, stupid, lazy. I can feel the hatred in it, you know? I want to get rid of it, to stop it.

THERAPIST: Yes, it's a painful experience – you've just let yourself have food, which you very much need, and then the voice comes and punishes you. I'm wondering, though... that voice... what do you think it's trying to do?

SAM: Well, I think if I didn't have the voice I'd probably start eating and never stop. I imagine that sometimes – just sitting down and eating 15 donuts. If I let myself start like that, then I'd probably never stop.

THERAPIST: Yes, so there's a part of you that feels insatiable, which isn't surprising, because you're malnourished. But there may be more there...

SAM: Even if I weren't malnourished, part of me would want to keep eating. It would never be enough. As we're talking about it, I can see how terrifying that is to me – the idea that I'd never get enough.

In this excerpt, Sam and I are beginning to talk about a conflict he experiences between the part of him that feels an overpowering desire for food and another part of himself that harshly restrains these impulses. In the drive-conflict model, this scenario reflects Sam's attempts to manage his overpowering oral libidinal impulses through denial and the restrictions of his superego. Ongoing therapeutic work will seek to help Sam to develop a gentler and more tolerant superego (Schafer, 1960), to find a way to respectfully acknowledge his desires and strike a balance between need and excess.

Sam's overpowering desire for food certainly reflects his intense need for it in his malnourished state. Yet we are also discovering that the intensity of his desire for food has symbolic meanings. With this in mind, Sam and I explore the symbolic, relational, and familial meanings of food and eating in an effort to understand his experience of intense desire for food in the following excerpt:

SAM: I think my mother really tried to be there for me. She'd get up and make breakfast on Saturdays, even though she looked sad and exhausted. But she never made it through the day. She was always in bed again by noon.

THERAPIST: When you were young, how did you understand your mother's returning to bed? Can you get ahold of what you might have thought about that when you were a child at all?

SAM: I knew something was wrong, that maybe she was sad. What I remember the most is sitting in the living room waiting for her to get out of bed. It was just me, by myself, and it would seem like Saturday afternoons were endless. I was so bored and alone and the tension of waiting would build and build...

THERAPIST: That tension, that anxiety, of waiting for your mother to get up, to see that she was okay and available to you, was impossible to manage alone.

SAM: I hated myself for wanting her so badly when she had almost nothing left to give. And so I'd get a bag of chips to numb myself. It's familiar.

In this excerpt, we learn that for Sam food was an early maternal substitute, providing comfort and dependability in contrast to his mother, who was often unavailable. Sam's desire for food reflects his malnourished state but also the intense desire of a young child who needed his mother's comfort. As this scenario repeated, food also became linked with Sam's anger toward a "needy and dependent" part of himself that so desperately wanted his mother's comfort. Indeed, in the act of eating Sam was, we discovered, both comforting and punishing a frightened and vulnerable part of himself.

Object Relations Model

Shifting emphasis from Freud's drive-conflict model of the mind, the object relations model emphasizes the psyche's need to integrate various representations of self and important others. The object relations model emphasizes what the primary people, or objects, were like in a person's early environment, and how they were experienced, transformed, and internalized as internal objects. Internal objects function in relationship to each other and to external objects, or people in the environment. Indeed, this model describes how people in an individual's life were experienced during childhood and how internal representations of those people continue to color unconscious life in the present moment (McWilliams, 1994)

Hilde Bruch was the first person to describe anorexia nervosa in the language of object relations. Challenging the drive-conflict model of anorexia nervosa, Bruch emphasized more primitive factors that resulted in the deficits in autonomy and self-identity in patients with anorexia nervosa (Swift, 1991). Bruch and the object relations theorist who followed cited disturbances in the early mother–child relationship that predispose the child to develop the disorder during adolescence (Humphrey, 1991). In her observations of patients with anorexia nervosa, Bruch described over-involved caretakers who were domineering, intrusive, and discouraging of separation and individuation.

In contrast to the drive-conflict theorists, Bruch recognized the existence of men and boys with anorexia nervosa. In a seminal study of nine male patients with anorexia nervosa, Bruch (1971) observed a pattern where a controlling adult, usually the mother, imposed on her developing child her own concepts of the child's needs and desires. This enmeshed dynamic ran smoothly until the children reached adolescence, when their demand for separation and individuation disrupted the status quo.

Children who grow up with over-involved caretakers, according to Bruch (1971), function well until a situation demands independent decision making and self-initiated behavior. Bruch observed that boys with anorexia nervosa were almost always success- and achievement-oriented. Many were intensely interested in athletics. These boys had also received a great deal of encouragement from their families, teachers, and even peers for being outstanding. In many cases, the onset of anorexia nervosa began when their superior status was threatened, or when they began to have serious doubts about their competence. Although their parents were able to compensate for the strain of excessive performance through careful planning in the past, at a certain point – usually late pre-adolescence – as the children formed important extra-familial relationships, this became impossible. The children were confronted with the limits of their own competence.

At this point, anorexia nervosa began to serve an adaptive function for these children, as an effort to take charge of themselves. However, changes in the body and its size cannot provide a real sense of self-directed identity, and their pursuit of thinness became increasingly frantic and extreme. At the same time, self-starvation is an oppositional behavior that, at the superficial level, disrupts the symbiotic relationship between caretaker and child (Johnson, 1991). Self-starvation was an attempt to both develop autonomy and defend against further maternal intrusiveness.

The over-involved caretaker's ability to respond to the child is determined more by the caretaker's needs than those of the child (Johnson, 1991). According to Bruch (1971), this pattern interrupts the child's developing ability to identify and articulate internal states. Children are active participants in their development. They experience a diffuse need (e.g., hunger) that is communicated with a signal (e.g., crying). It is up to the caretaker to empathically decode that signal and respond appropriately. A child's ability to differentiate his internal states is facilitated or stunted by his caretaker's ability to correctly decode and appropriately respond to his communication. Because in children with anorexia nervosa this ability is interfered with by an over-involved caretaker, their ability to identify and articulate internal states is compromised (Johnson, 1991). Indeed, research shows that adolescent patients with anorexia nervosa are less expressive than adolescents without the disorder (Felker & Stivers, 1994).

A number of other object relations formulations of anorexia nervosa have been proposed, emphasizing distortions in representations of the body, self, and objects. For example, Masterson (1978) argued that the patient with anorexia nervosa has an internal maternal object that becomes hostile and rejecting as the patient moves toward separation and individuation and another that becomes supportive and rewarding in response to dependent, clinging behavior. Each of these internal representations of the mother has its corresponding self-representation – the first as bad, empty, and guilty and the second as passive, compliant, and good. Working together, these internal objects undermine the patient's attempts at separation and individuation, which is seen as incompatible with the symptoms and behavior of anorexia nervosa.

Humphrey (1991) argued that patients with anorexia nervosa have experienced failures in the early holding environment. Winnicott's (1965) metaphor of the mother–infant holding environment refers to three capacities that a "good enough" mother provides during the first years of her child's life. First, the mother nurtures the child, both in the physical sense of an environment where the child can eat, sleep, and grow to its full potential, and, equally important, in the emotional sense. Second, the mother soothes and regulates tension by tolerating and containing the child's intense affect. Third, the mother responds to the child's fluctuating need for closeness and distance in a genuinely empathic way, while affirming the child's identity as a separate person.

According to Humphrey (1991), caretakers of children with anorexia nervosa lack one or more of the three capacities a good enough mother provides during the early years of life. First, in families with a child that has anorexia nervosa, both caretaker and child may be starved for emotional warmth. In some cases, the caretaker provides nurturance in abundance as long as the child remains dependent. Once the child begins to separate and individuate, however, they are negated, abandoned, or even punished. Second, the family, especially the caretaker–child dyad, may be unable to regulate tension and tolerate negative emotion. As a result, the family is constricted, superficial, and denying, much like the individual with anorexia nervosa themself.

Third, genuine empathy between caretaker and child requires that the caretaker "mirror" the child's "spontaneous gesture" (Winnicott, 1965) or "signal" of emerging individuality, instead of imposing rigid expectations from the outside. Because the caretaker of a patient with anorexia nervosa may still be struggling with separation and individuation from their own parents, they are unable to facilitate this process in the child. Instead, the caretaker experiences the spontaneous gesture as a threat to the stability and well-being of the family, and especially to their own enmeshment with the child. The emerging self of the child is enfeebled by invalidating and rejecting responses to separation and individuation, combined with solicitation of more dependent behavior.

As Sam and I continue our work together, we notice a pattern. When I am scheduled to have time away from the office for vacation, Sam's restrictive eating intensifies. In the following excerpt, we explore the nature of this dynamic between us and its relation to Sam's internal object world.

THERAPIST: I think it's worth noting that these restrictive eating behaviors are showing up right before the week-long break we'll be having soon. I'm wondering if that's occurred to you and what your thoughts are about it.

SAM: It's fine – not a big deal.

THERAPIST: Yes, it's hard to speak to the ways that it might be hard to not have these meetings, which I think you do depend on.

SAM: I guess I do depend on them. But then people aren't always available when you need them, are they? You have to make do.

THERAPIST: That was the situation you found yourself in as a child. The fact that I'm leaving even though you depend on me to help you navigate these difficult times puts you in the same spot that you were in when you were small and your mother would go back to bed early in the day, leaving you alone to manage your anxiety without the help you needed.

SAM: YEAH. I guess I'm a little mad at you, but then I also feel guilty about being mad at you. You deserve to have a vacation, too.

In this excerpt, Sam and I begin to explore the way that his historical relationship with his mother colors his relationship with me, his therapist. Sam has come to rely on the therapeutic relationship in much the same way that a child relies on the holding environment provided by his caretaker. And through our shared inquiry, we discover that my upcoming vacation echoes the situation in which he found himself as a child, needing to rely on food-based coping mechanisms to deal with his mother's absence.

Self Psychology Model

Self psychology begins with the work of Kohut (1971), who argued that the capacity to tolerate separation from important others, beginning with the first caretaker, without falling apart depends on particular psychic functions. These functions, which he termed *selfobject functions*, include the capacity to provide one's own sense of cohesiveness, self-soothing, vitality, realistic self-esteem, and tension regulation. In Kohut's view, these functions were originally provided by a caretaking figure, most often the mother.

While the child relies on the caretaker to provide selfobject functions at first, over time the child increasingly makes use of a transitional object, instead of only the mother, to serve this role. Transitional objects, such as blankets or stuffed toys, fall under the child's full control. While they are cognitively perceived as part of the external world, transitional objects are emotionally experienced as a part of the self (Winnicott, 1953). As development unfolds in a good enough way, the child's ability to perform his own selfobject functions is consolidated and the transitional object is forgotten.

Contemporary infant research also throws light on the growing child's internalization of selfobject functions. Indeed, from the earliest stages of life, the child participates in a bidirectional process of communication, both verbal and nonverbal, with the primary caretaker. This communication provides emotional regulation and impacts both caretaker and child over time (Beebe & Lachman, 2002). In this paradigm, feeding is understood as one of the most important early experiences of mutual regulation. When the caretaker has difficulty in recognizing, empathically responding to, and meeting the child's needs, the child's developing capacities for self-regulation are deeply impacted and their growing selfobject functions are impaired.

The self psychological model emphasizes that symptoms of anorexia nervosa may represent attempts to restore cohesion and vitality to self-experience. While symptoms may have symbolic meaning, in this model they more importantly serve to reinforce aspects of the self that are threatened or damaged. For example, the patient may be driven to frenetic activity, often in the form of compulsive exercise, in an effort to avoid underlying feelings of emptiness, boredom, and despair. Similarly, by repetitively counting calories and regulating food intake, the patient narrows their experience of the world to a size that is more manageable. These and other aspects of anorexia nervosa provide a means of emotional regulation, bypassing reliance on relational ties, which are experienced as unreliable and even dangerous. As the disorder continues to develop, it may provide the patient with a compensatory identity and accompanying feelings of significance in a world experienced as threatening insignificance (Goodsitt, 1997).

Much later in Sam's treatment, after his shoulder injury has healed and weight restoration has been achieved, his physician and nutritionist permit him to return to a less strenuous version of his exercise regimen. In the process, important psychological dynamics are unearthed and become the topic of our conversations.

SAM: It's so hard for me to stop. When it's time to leave the gym, I feel really angry that I'm supposed to leave. The endorphins, the focus.
THERAPIST: Being at the gym takes you away from the sadness we've been talking about, the depression.
SAM: Yeah, it really does. All day long I'm anticipating getting to the gym. I'm so focused on getting there it's like I'm barely at school. And then because of these stupid restrictions I have to leave, even though only an hour has passed.
THERAPIST: If you can get ahold of it, what would you be feeling at school if you weren't thinking about the gym?
SAM: The first word that comes to mind is terror, which doesn't make a lot of sense. I don't know why I'd feel terror at school. But it does feel true. The anxiety is really overwhelming... like I'm going to explode.

In this excerpt, we can see how being at the gym and even thinking about the gym, in a driven and obsessive way, serves to counteract Sam's intense anxiety. As the self psychological model emphasizes, anxiety is fundamentally a threat to the integrity of the self. When there are extreme deficits in the cohesion and differentiation of the self structure, experiences of threat may lead to the dissolution of the self (Kohut, 1977). For Sam, compulsive and driven exercise represents an attempt to restore cohesion to self-experience. In our treatment, I seek to provide selfobject functions to Sam with the hope that, over time, he can internalize them as his own. Indeed, our goal is for Sam to develop a greater sense of his own cohesiveness, realistic self-esteem, and the capacity for more effective regulation of his emotional experience.

Psychosexual Development

Early on, researchers suggested that sexual development plays an important role in male anorexia nervosa. Research suggests that males with eating disorders are significantly more likely to have had no sexual relations and to report being homosexual (Burns & Crisp, 1985). Ultimately, most adolescents with anorexia nervosa lose their sexual drive (Crisp & Burns, 1983; Hall, Delahunt, & Ellis, 1985; Carlat, Camargo, & Herzog, 1997). In part, this is a result of diminished levels of testosterone and other sex-related hormones (Herzog, Bradburn, & Newman, 1990). For more information on this aspect of male anorexia nervosa, see Chapter 5: The Biological Metaframework.

Diminished sexual desire has an important secondary gain for many males with anorexia nervosa. Indeed, consistent with clinical experience, Crisp and Burns (1983) noted that few males with anorexia nervosa complain about their lack of sexual drive. Crisp (1967) suggested that the reduction of libido secondary to weight loss facilitates a withdrawal from adolescent maturational conflicts. Romero (1994) stated that many males with anorexia nervosa are retreating from the pressure to establish a male sexual identity. One possibility is that gender identity confusion increases their sensitivity to fat development because of its association to the feminine shape (Crisp & Burns, 1990). This possibility is discussed in more detail in Chapter 6: The Cultural Metaframework.

Similarly, researchers have suggested that some males with anorexia nervosa experience pre-morbid homosexual panic (Crisp, 1967; Dally & Gomez, 1979). As their sexuality begins to take shape, males may be frightened by attraction to other males, and the elimination of sexual desire achieved through severe weight loss may protect them from confronting this fact. However, this hypothesis is not applicable to all males with anorexia nervosa; indeed, in my clinical experience some young men attempt extreme weight loss in an attempt to become more sexually attractive to other males. The relationship between male anorexia nervosa and homosexuality is discussed in more detail in Chapter 6: The Culture and Gender Metaframework.

In the next chapter, we turn to the development of a metaframework that captures the spiritual component of anorexia nervosa in men and boys. Acknowledging the fact that anorexia nervosa is deeply related to spirituality, we begin with a short case excerpt. In particular, we explore the possibilities for treatment of anorexia nervosa in men and boys that incorporate mindfulness and yoga. We discuss the central role of forgiveness in treatment and, finally, the possibility of posttraumatic growth.

References

Beebe, B. & Lachman, F. (2002). *Infant research and adult treatment: Co-constructing interactions.* Hillsdale, NJ: The Analytic Press.

Berlin, I. N., Boatman, M. J., Scheimo, S. L., & Szurek, S. A. (1951). Adolescent alternation of anorexia and obesity. *American Journal of Orthopsychiatry*, *21*, 387–419.

Bruch, H. (1971). Anorexia nervosa in the male. *Psychosomatic Medicine*, *35*(1), 31–47.

Burns, T. & Crisp, A. H. (1985). Factors affecting prognosis in male anorexics. *Journal of Psychiatric Research*, *19*, 323–328.

Carlat, D. J., Carmago, C. A., & Herzog, D. B. (1997). Eating disorders in males: A report on 135 patients. *American Journal of Psychiatry*, *154* (8), 1127–1131.

Crisp, A. H. (1967). The possible significance of some behavioural correlates of weight and carbohydrate intake. *Journal of Psychosomatic Research*, *11*(1), 117–131.

Crisp, A. H. & Burns, T. (1983). The clinical presentation of anorexia nervosa in males. *International Journal of Eating Disorders*, *2*(4), 5–10.

Crisp, A. H. & Burns, T. (1990). Primary anorexia nervosa in the male and female: A comparison of clinical features and prognosis. In A. E. Andersen (Ed.), *Males with eating disorders* (pp. 77–99). New York: Brunner/Mazel.

Dally, P. & Gomez, J. (1979). *Anorexia nervosa.* New York: William Heinemann Medical Books.

Felker, K. R. & Stivers, C. (1994). The relationship of gender and family environment to eating disorder risk in adolescents. *Adolescence*, *29*(116), 821–834.

Freud, S. (1961). *The ego and the id.* In J. Strachey (Ed. and Trans.), *The standard edition of the complete psychological works of Sigmund Freud* (Vol. 19, pp. 3–66). London: Hogarth Press. (Original work published 1923.)

Goodsitt, A. (1997). Eating disorders: A self-psychological perspective. In D. M. Garner & P. E. Garfinkel (Eds.), *Handbook of treatment for eating disorders* (2nd ed.). New York: The Guilford Press.

Hall, A., Delahunt, J. W., & Ellis, P. (1985). Anorexia nervosa in the male: Clinical features and follow-up of nine patients. *Journal of Psychiatric Research*, *19*, 315–321.

Herzog, D. B., Bradburn, I. S., & Newman, K. (1990). Sexuality in males with eating disorders. In A. E. Andersen (Ed.), *Males with eating disorders* (pp. 40–53). New York: Brunner/Mazel.

Humphrey, L. L. (1991). Object relations and the family system: An integrative approach to understanding and treating eating disorders. In C. Johnson (Ed.), *Psychodynamic treatment of anorexia nervosa and bulimia* (pp. 51–67). New York: The Guilford Press.

Johnson, C. L. (1991). Treatment of eating disordered patients with borderline and false-self/narcissistic disorders. In C. Johnson (Ed.), *Psychodynamic treatment of anorexia nervosa and bulimia* (pp. 165–193). New York: The Guilford Press.

Kohut, H. (1971). *The analysis of the self: A systematic approach to the psychoanalytic treatment of narcissistic personality disorders.* New York: International Universities Press, Inc.

Kohut, H. (1977). *The restoration of the self.* New York: International Universities Press.

Masserman, J. H. (1941). Psychodynamisms in anorexia nervosa and neurotic vomiting. *Psychoanalytic Quarterly, 10,* 211–242.

Masterson, J. F. (1978). Paradise lost – bulimia, a closet narcissistic personality disorder: A developmental self and object relations approach. In R. C. Marohn & S. C. Feinstein (Eds.), *Adolescent psychiatry (*Vol 20, pp. 253–266). New York: Analytic Press.

McWilliams, N. (1994). *Psychoanalytic diagnosis: Understanding personality structure in the clinical process.* New York: The Guilford Press.

Moulton, R. (1942). A psychosomatic study of anorexia nervosa including the use of vaginal smears. *Psychosomatic Medicine, 4,* 62–74.

Romero, F. (1994). Adolescent boys and anorexia nervosa. *Adolescence, 29*(115), 643–647.

Rowland, C. V. (1970). Anorexia nervosa: A survey of the literature and review of 30 cases. *International Psychiatric Clinics, 7,* 37–137.

Schafer, R. (1960). The loving and beloved superego in Freud's structural theory. *Psychoanalytic Study of the Child, 15,* 163–188.

Swift, W. J. (1991). Bruch revisited: The role of interpretation of transference and resistance in the psychotherapy of eating disorders. In C. Johnson (Ed.), *Psychodynamic treatment of anorexia nervosa and bulimia* (pp. 51–67). New York: The Guilford Press.

Waller, J. V., Kaufman, M. R., & Deutsch, F. (1940). Anorexia nervosa: Psychosomatic entity. *Psychosomatic Medicine, 2,* 3–16.

Winnicott, D. W. (1953). Transitional objects and transitional phenomena: A study of the first not-me possession. *The International Journal of Psychoanalysis, 34,* 89–97.

Winnicott, D. W. (1965). *The maturational processes and the facilitating environment: Studies in the theory of emotional development.* London: The Hogarth Press.

9 The Spiritual Metaframework

Pete is a 23-year-old graduate student who comes to me because he hasn't yet been able to establish a fulfilling intimate relationship. As I learn in our first interview, Pete struggled throughout his adolescence with anorexia nervosa, reaching a medically dangerous low weight and frequently purging after meals, before his family insisted that he attend treatment. Now, Pete feels proud of his recovery, having maintained a healthy body weight for several years without relapsing into symptomatic behavior.

Yet Pete remains troubled. Early on, I notice that he attends many of our twice-weekly sessions dressed in gym clothes with his yoga mat in tow. When I ask about his yoga practice, he tells me that yoga has been essential in helping him to develop a more positive body image and to experience his body "as living, breathing, and powerful" instead of as an object to be controlled. Through his spiritual practice of yoga, Pete has developed a new and more positive relationship with his body.

It was not until months later that Pete was able to talk with me about the more difficult aspects of his spiritual practice. In fact, Pete practices so-called "hot yoga," in which difficult poses are performed in a room heated to 105 degrees. And Pete does yoga every day and, on weekends, sometimes attends up to four classes. While recognizing the value of Pete's commitment to spiritual practice, I also attempt to highlight the parallels between his yoga practice and his history with anorexia nervosa.

PETE: I think the thing I like about yoga is that I feel so... the best way I can describe it is "clean"... afterwards.

THERAPIST: Clean – that's an evocative word. What's it like to feel clean?

PETE: It's really hard to describe, you know. There's something about the moments after the yoga class, when I'm totally spent... exhausted... there's nothing coming up for me, I'm still and empty in a way. I might even describe it as numb, though that doesn't sound very good.

THERAPIST: Empty and numb – like purging as an adolescent.

PETE: Ugh. It is like that in a lot of ways. And if I miss a yoga class, I feel so anxious... the same way I feel after eating a big

meal, that feeling that drove me to purge in the first place…
butterflies in my stomach…

As we can see from this excerpt, Pete is heavily relying on hot yoga
as a way to regulate his emotional and somatic experience. Indeed, the
experience of hot yoga, which leaves him "too exhausted to feel anything,"
as he later described it, functions as a healthier (albeit rigid and socially
isolating) means of flattening the textures of his emotional life, in contrast
to his prior reliance on purging and restrictive eating.

Pete's yoga practice contains an important movement toward health.
In embracing his interest in spirituality, he is acknowledging an aspect of
himself that strives toward a greater experience of personal wholeness. For
patients with a history of anorexia nervosa, this is a significant milestone.
And the struggles that men encounter in embracing their spirituality take
a particular shape. Many men would categorize the spiritual, with its
emphasis on acknowledging and expressing their deepest layers of joy,
sensitivity, and pain, as at odds with the masculine (Fox, 1998). In finding
yoga, Pete has found a means of making contact with these deeper layers
of his mind and body.

Yet, at the same time, Pete's spiritual pursuits are marked by the same
difficulties in managing his emotional experience that drove him to
disordered eating as an adolescent. Ultimately, the task of psychotherapy
is to understand and lift the constraints that prevent Pete from more fully
embracing his spiritual life in all its complexity.

Pete's questions are not unique. In my clinical practice, I find that young
men (and women) are continually struggling with spiritual questions.
Adolescence has been described as a time of "spiritual awakening" (Cobb,
Kor, & Miller, 2015). In fact, anorexia nervosa has a spiritual component.
As Andersen (2014) pointed out, the core of eating disorders includes a
profoundly spiritual element. How is it that an otherwise healthy male,
most often in the prime of adolescence, becomes so profoundly unhappy
that they reject a crucial aspect of their humanity – their body? Indeed, as
men and boys struggle to establish their identities, and a corresponding
sense of what is most important, some fixate on their bodies, neglecting
their developing inner emotional worlds.

Spirituality is an inclusive term that describes several aspects of human
experience, including a relationship with God or a higher power, a sense
of relationship and interconnection (Griffith & Griffith, 2002), meaning
and purpose in life, and a sense of value and morality (Fukuyama,
Puig, Baggs, & Wolf, 2014). While spiritual concerns take many forms
and depend on factors ranging from cultural background to personal
aptitudes, in this chapter we take up three aspects of spirituality that
dovetail with the treatment of anorexia nervosa and frequently arise in
clinical practice: mindfulness and yoga, forgiveness, and the possibility
of posttraumatic growth.

Mindfulness and Yoga

Mindfulness is the ability to be present to one's unfolding, immediate experience and to attend to that experience with non-judgmental acceptance (Bishop et al., 2004; Baer, Smith, Hopkins, Krietemeyer, & Toney, 2006). As a dispositional feature, it has been described as "a receptive state of mind in which attention, informed by a sensitive awareness of what is occurring in the present, simply observes what is taking place" (Brown & Ryan, 2003).

It has been suggested that mindfulness is a gateway to both increased spiritual awareness and a more integrated spiritual life. In this way, mindfulness may be particularly appealing to adolescents, who are often deeply involved in negotiating their spiritual lives (Cobb, Kor, & Miller, 2015). Equally important, mindfulness appears to positively affect many interrelated psychological functions, including self-awareness and emotional self-regulation (Brown & Ryan, 2003). Because of this, mindfulness has been integrated with several broad treatment approaches.

With the rise of "third wave" therapies such as acceptance and commitment therapy, dialectical behavior therapy, and mindfulness-based cognitive therapy, clinicians increasingly emphasize mindful attention to body-based processes such as the experience of emotion and physical sensation, in contrast to the largely thought-driven analysis and verbal interpretation emphasized in earlier approaches. In this process, mindfulness-based therapies have received empirical validation for physiological disorders such as chronic pain (Elomaa, de C Williams, & Kalso, 2009), fibromyalgia (Lush et al., 2009) and chronic fatigue syndrome (Surawy, Roberts, & Silver, 2005) as well as for psychological disorders including anxiety disorders (Davis, Strasburger, & Brown, 2007), mood disorders (Segal, Williams, & Teasdale, 2002), addictions (Hsu, Grow, & Marlatt, 2008), sleep disorders (Ong, Shapiro, & Manber, 2008), and trauma symptoms (Batten, Orsillo, & Walser, 2005).

More recently, research has begun to emerge showing the potential application of mindfulness-based therapies in the treatment of eating disorders (Wanden-Berghe, Sanz-Valero, & Wanden-Berghe, 2011). For example, individuals with eating disorders have been shown to exhibit lower levels of dispositional mindfulness than their healthy peers (Lavander, Jardin, & Anderson, 2009). Furthermore, it has been suggested that offering mindfulness-based interventions may have a preventative effect on the development of eating disorders (Proulx, 2005).

Anorexia nervosa has been described as an illness of psychological inflexibility, an inability to behave in flexible and creative ways in the presence of difficult thoughts, feelings, and bodily sensations (Merwin et al., 2010). In fact, it has been shown that individuals with anorexia nervosa have less psychological flexibility than their recovered counterparts who, in turn, have less psychological flexibility than healthy controls (Merwin et al., 2010). This accords with clinical experience, which shows that patients who have achieved full symptom remission retain problematic psychological dynamics. It has been suggested that mindfulness- and acceptance-based treatments may provide a useful way of addressing the psychological inflexibility characteristic of patients with anorexia nervosa (Merwin et al., 2010).

This psychological inflexibility takes a particular shape in the relationship that patients with anorexia nervosa establish with their bodies. Indeed, the body is not subject to precise manipulation. With innumerable variables contributing to its state at any moment, it defies our omnipotent manipulation. Those who lack the capacity to tolerate this ongoing flux may resort to desperate attempts to force homeostasis, whether through fasting, excessive exercise, or other means of flattening their experience of bodily aliveness. Similarly, behavioral symptoms such as weight checking and calorie counting provide a refuge from bodily unpredictability and change (Merwin et al., 2010).

Similarly, psychological inflexibility leaves its mark on mental life. The symptoms of anorexia nervosa provide a sense of predictability, safety, and control by providing clear rules for behavior, bypassing emotional experiences, which are experienced as confusing and messy. These rules tell the patient what, when, and how much to eat. With attention captured by these rules, patients are less likely to attend to their internal emotional experience. Ultimately, significant weight loss and prolonged starvation profoundly flatten the patient's emotional life by numbing the body. Indeed, increased parasympathetic activation (Miller, Redlich, & Steiner, 2003), among other physiological changes, has been shown to reduce the intensity of affect (Craig, 2004). Similarly, hunger cues fade away as starvation continues (Wang, Hung, & Randall, 2006).

Mindfulness may provide one means of counteracting psychological inflexibility. As patients learn to observe an experience as it unfolds in the present moment, they develop the capacity to observe their bodily experience with increased equanimity, to step back from rigid reliance on behavioral rules, and to tolerate and learn from their emotional experience. Over time, patients may develop an increased ability to integrate their emotional experience into decision making about food as well as in a broad range of others domains. At present, there is preliminary data confirming mindfulness as a mediator between the thinking characteristic of patients with anorexia nervosa and the disorder's accompanying behavior (Masuda, Price, Anderson, & Wendell, 2010).

As Pete and I explored the role of yoga practice in his spiritual life, we found that it was often used as a way to bypass difficult emotional experience.

PETE: This weekend I felt really depressed. After our therapy session on Friday, I couldn't stop thinking about how angry I

> am at my parents. But I went to the [yoga] studio on Saturday morning, and that helped... I felt peaceful for the rest of the day.

THERAPIST: It's a helpful resource... your yoga classes ... but I find myself wondering what happened to the anger that you were describing on Friday. Where did it go?

PETE: I don't know really. There's no room for it in yoga class. All of my attention is taken up by the poses – it's called one-pointed concentration. And afterwards, that feeling stays for a while.

THERAPIST: I find myself wondering about what's lost. In finding this calm state, it seems that you lose other thoughts and feelings that are important.

As we can see in this excerpt, yoga practice is providing a means for Pete to regulate his emotional experience. Through yoga, Pete can find a state of calm and peace; at the same time, we are beginning to wonder what other thoughts and feelings are bypassed through Pete's heavy reliance on yoga. Over time, Pete will make forays into restorative yoga, in which poses are held for a longer time and with less athletic exertion, as well as mindfulness practices as venues for contacting the full range of his emotional experience. Indeed, at its best, yoga has benefits for patients in recovery from eating disorders (Mitchell, Mazzeo, Rausch, & Cooke, 2007; McIver, O'Halloran, & McGartland, 2009) as well as a number of psychological disorders (Shannahoff-Khalsa, 2004; da Silva, Ravindran, & Ravindran, 2009). Because of this, yoga is increasingly used as an adjunctive form of treatment in many residential programs and in outpatient settings.

Forgiveness

The concept of forgiveness has been discussed since the beginning of recorded history and is an integral aspect of the world's philosophical and religious traditions (Griswold, 2007). In a wide-ranging literature, researchers have evaluated the impact of forgiveness on conditions ranging from depression, substance abuse, anxiety, relational problems, to eating disorders (Enright & Fitzgibbons, 2000). Forgiveness has also been linked to improved physiological health (Harris & Thoresen, 2005).

While forgiveness has been defined in a number of ways, here we conceive of forgiveness as a "prosocial change toward a perceived transgressor" (McCullough, Pargament, & Thoresen, 2000). This definition entails that patients begin to think differently about the offender and offense. In this process, patients consider concepts such as intent, responsibility, and severity to interpret the nature of the offense and to understand how the offender should be perceived and interacted with

(Weick, 1995). As forgiveness takes place, patients experience a changing affective relationship to the offender, which entails decreased anger and increased empathy (Worthington, 2006).

Discussing the role of forgiveness in the treatment of anorexia nervosa is complex and depends on the nuances of each patient's experience. As recovery proceeds, patients naturally seek to understand the elements that gave rise to their struggle with food, weight, and shape. In this process, they often identify factors in the media and cultural surround that influenced their development in negative ways. In other cases, particular people may be identified as contributing to the patient's emotional struggles; for example, coaches or peers may have teased the patient, which, in combination with other factors, contributed to the onset of their disordered eating.

Perhaps most difficult, however, is the anger that is often directed towards family members and, of course, parents in particular. It has been noted that relational proximity increases the impetus to forgive (Fehr, Gelfand, & Nag, 2010) and, thus, forgiveness takes on particular importance as patients continue active involvement with their families. In my clinical practice, patients often struggle to understand the development of their illness. In many cases, we identify factors in the family that may have contributed to its development. This recognition is almost always accompanied by intense anger which may, at times, be masked by other symptoms such as guilt, self-blame, and depression. In most cases, these feelings coexist with feelings of love, gratitude, and dependency. As treatment proceeds, patients struggle to reconcile these feelings.

When Pete mentioned his parents early in treatment, I was struck by the distance and aloofness that characterized their relationship. Indeed, Pete appeared to have good reason for maintaining this distance, describing his mother as crippled by her anxiety and his father as intrusive and domineering. Pete's aloofness from his family seemed, however, to mask his significant feelings of anger and frustration as well as his longing for a deeper connection. As Pete increasingly gave voice to his rage, he also began to engage more directly with his parents. While these interactions were often disappointing, over time Pete spoke of the importance of compassion in his spiritual practice and began to attempt to extend this compassion to his parents. At the same time, Pete worked to maintain a complex understanding of his parents, including both their strengths and limitations.

Indeed, as anger is given room for its full expression, patients often begin to access increased empathy and compassion, including an appreciation of how significant others have been shaped by difficulties in their own families. In many cases, patients begin to recognize the other's positive intent in spite of the difficulties that may have developed in implementation. Ultimately, it is hoped that patients will be able to relate to the other in their full complexity, which includes gratitude for the positive things that the other was able to offer as well as recognition of the other's limitations.

Posttraumatic Growth

The world's religious traditions, including the ideas of the ancient Hebrews, Greeks, and early Christians, as well as teachings of Hinduism, Buddhism, and Islam all recognize the potentially transformative power of pain and suffering (Tedeschi & Calhoun, 1995). In recent years, clinicians and researchers, too, are increasingly recognizing the possibility of psychological growth following stress and trauma. Attempting to capture and investigate this idea, Calhoun and Tedeschi (1999) coined the term *posttraumatic growth* and argued that it may occur in at least three important ways: changes in the perception of self, changes in relating to others, and philosophical changes of priorities, appreciation, and spirituality.

Not everyone who experiences stress or trauma grows as a result of it. In the literature, three factors have been identified as central to determining whether posttraumatic growth will occur. First, the person in question must experience enough distress to initiate the cognitive processes needed for growth (Levine, Laufer, Hamama-Raz, Stein, & Solomon, 2008). Second, social support, which involves being able to talk about the trauma in the context of an emotionally supportive relationship, is an important component in determining whether posttraumatic growth takes place (Werdel, Dy-Liacco, Ciarrocchi, Wicks, & Breslford, 2014). Third, personality factors such as extraversion and openness to new experiences increase the likelihood of posttraumatic growth (Calhoun & Tedeschi, 1999).

Notably, research suggests that women experience greater posttraumatic growth than their male counterparts (Vishnevsky, Cann, Calhoun, Tedeschi, & Demakis, 2010). While the reason for this remains uncertain, we might speculate that women are more likely to make use of social support, which is a key factor in determining whether posttraumatic growth will occur. Regardless, if we conceive of anorexia nervosa as deeply stressful and traumatic, these findings highlight the important role that psychotherapy may play in the long-term process of rehabilitation and recovery. We see this in the following excerpt.

PETE: I've been thinking a lot about this. You know, in the same way I deserve to feed myself well, I also deserve to feel all of myself. I was talking about this with my girlfriend – how it's so hard for me to take in good things. But I think I'm learning to do that more and more.

THERAPIST: Yes, you're talking about how you deserve nourishment, and how you're still figuring out what that exactly means.

PETE: But maybe that's what yoga is really about, you know? About finding a way in this world to be in touch with myself, instead of controlling my experience – whether it's food or feelings or whatever.

In this excerpt, Pete struggles with understanding the impact of anorexia nervosa on his sense of self, his relationship with others, and on his spiritual and philosophical orientation toward living. In particular, Pete links these changes directly to his spiritual practice, which has been an ongoing topic in our treatment. Indeed, research suggests that posttraumatic growth is linked to religious and spiritual practices (Cadell, Regehr, & Hemsworth, 2003). Because of this, Pete's yoga practice is an important resource as he navigates the latter stages of recovery. By including the spiritual aspect of a patient's experience, in addition to emphasizing the importance of weight recovery and symptom remission, we take advantage of an important opportunity to assist patients in the longer-term process of re-ordering their lives in profound and lasting ways.

References

Andersen, A. (2014). A brief history of eating disorders in males. In L. Cohn & R. Lemberg (Eds.), *Current findings on males with eating disorders* (pp. 4–10). New York: Routledge.

Baer, R. A., Smith, G. T., Hopkins, J., Krietemeyer, J., & Toney, L. (2006). Using self-report assessment methods to explore facts of mindfulness. *Assessment*, 13(1), 27–45.

Batten, S. V., Orsillo, S. M., & Walser, R. D. (2005). Acceptance and mindfulness-based approaches to the treatment of posttraumatic stress disorder. In S. M. Orsillo & L. Roemer (Eds.), *Acceptance and mindfulness-based approaches to anxiety: Conceptualization and treatment* (pp. 241–270). New York: Springer.

Bishop, S. R., Lau, M. A., Shapiro, S. L., Carlson, L., Anderson, N. D., Carmody, J., ... Devins, G. (2004). Mindfulness: A proposed operational definition. *Clinical Psychology*, *11*, 230–241.

Brown K. W. & Ryan, R. M. (2003). The benefits of being present: Mindfulness and its role in psychological well-being. *Journal of Personality and Social Psychology*, *84*(4), 822–848.

Cadell, S., Regehr, C., & Hemsworth, D. (2003). Factors contributing to posttraumatic growth: A proposed structural equation model. *American Journal of Orthopsychiatry*, *73*, 279–287.

Calhoun, L. J. & Tedeschi, R. G. (1999). *Facilitating posttraumatic growth: A clinician's guide*. Mahwah, NJ: Lawrence Erlbaum Associates, Inc.

Cobb, E., Kor, A., & Miller, L. (2015). Support for adolescent spirituality: Contributions of religious practice and trait mindfulness. *Journal of Religion and Health*, *54*(3), 862–870.

Craig, A. D. (2004). Human feelings: Why are some more aware than others? *Trends in Cognitive Sciences*, *8*, 239–241.

da Silva, T. L., Ravindran, L. N., & Ravindran, A. V. (2009). Yoga in the treatment of mood and anxiety disorders: A review. *Asian Journal of Psychiatry*, *2*(1), 6–16.

Davis, L. W., Strasburger, A. M., & Brown, L. F. (2007). Mindfulness: An intervention for anxiety in schizophrenia. *Journal of Psychosocial Nursing and Mental Health Services*, *45*(11), 23–29.

Elomaa, M. M., de C Williams, A. C., & Kalso, E. A. (2009). Attention management as a treatment for chronic pain. *European Journal of Pain*, *13*(10), 1062–1067.

Enright, R. D. & Fitzgibbons, R. P. (2000). *Helping clients forgive: An empirical guide for resolving anger and restoring hope.* Washington, DC: American Psychological Association.

Fehr, R., Gelfand, M. J., & Nag, M. (2010). The road to forgiveness: A meta-analytic synthesis of its situational and dispositional correlates. *Psychological Bulletin*, *136*(5), 894–914.

Fox, M. (1998). *The hidden spirituality of men: Ten metaphors to awaken the sacred masculine.* Novato, CA: New World Library.

Fukuyama, M., Puig, A., Baggs, A., & Wolf, C. P. (2014). Religion and spirituality. In F. T. Leong, L. Comas-Diaz, H. Nagayama, C. Gordon, V. McLoyd, & J. E. Trimble (Eds.), *APA handbook of multicultural psychology, Vol 1: Theory and research* (pp. 519–534). Washington, DC: American Psychological Association.

Griffith, J. L. & Griffith, M. E. (2002). *Encountering the sacred in psychotherapy: How to talk with people about their spiritual lives.* New York: Guilford Press.

Griswold, C. (2007). *Forgiveness: A philosophical exploration.* New York: Cambridge University Press.

Harris, A. H. & Thoresen, C. E. (2005). Volunteering is associated with delayed mortality in older people: Analysis of the longitudinal study of aging. *Journal of Health Psychology*, *10*(6), 739–752.

Hsu, S. H., Grow, J., & Marlatt, G. A. (2008). Mindfulness and addiction. *Recent Developments in Alcoholism*, *18*, 229–250.

Lavander J. M., Jardin B. F., & Anderson D. A. (2009). Bulimic symptoms in undergraduate men and women: Contributions of mindfulness and thought suppression. *Eating Behaviors*, *10*, 228–231.

Levine, S. Z., Laufer, A., Hamama-Raz, Y., Stein, E., & Solomon, Z. (2008). Posttraumatic growth in adolescence: Examining its components and relationship with PTSD. *Journal of Traumatic Stress*, *21*(5), 492–496.

Lush, E., Salmon, P., Floyd, A., Studts, J. L., Weissbecker, I., & Sephton, S. E. (2009). Mindfulness meditation for symptom reduction in fibromyalgia: Psychophysiological correlates. *Journal of Clinical Psychology in Medical Settings*, *16*(2), 200–207.

Masuda, A., Price, M., Anderson, P. L., & Wendell, J. W. (2010). Disordered eating-related cognition and psychological flexibility as predictors of psychological health among college students. *Behavior Modification*, *34*(1), 3–15.

McCullough, M. E., Pargament, K. I., & Thoresen, C. T. (Eds.). (2000). *Forgiveness: Theory, research, and practice.* New York: Guilford Press.

McIver, S., O'Halloran, P., & McGartland, M. (2009). Yoga as a treatment for binge eating disorder: A preliminary study. *Complementary Therapies in Medicine*, *17*(4), 196–202.

Merwin, R. M., Timko, C. A., Moskovich, A. A., Ingle, K. K., Bulik, C. M., & Zucker, N. L. (2010). Psychological inflexibility and symptom expression in anorexia nervosa. *Eating Disorders*, *19*(1), 62–82.

Miller, S. P., Redlich, A. D., & Steiner, H. (2003). The stress response in anorexia nervosa. *Child Psychiatry & Human Development, 33*(4), 295–306.

Mitchell, K. S., Mazzeo, S. E., Rausch, S. M., & Cooke, K. L. (2007). Innovative interventions for disordered eating: Evaluating dissonance based and yoga interventions. *International Journal of Eating Disorders, 40*(2), 120–128.

Ong, J. C., Shapiro, S. L., & Manber, R. (2008). Combining mindfulness meditation with cognitive-behavior therapy for insomnia: A treatment-development study. *Behavior Therapy, 39*(2), 171–182.

Proulx, K. (2005). Experiences of women with bulimia nervosa in a mindfulness-based eating disorder treatment group. *Eating Disorders: The Journal of Treatment & Prevention, 16*, 52–72.

Segal, Z. V., Williams, J. M. G., & Teasdale, J. D. (2002). *Mindfulness-based cognitive therapy for depression: A new approach to preventing relapse.* New York: The Guilford Press.

Shannahoff-Khalsa, D. S. (2004). An introduction to Kundalini yoga meditation techniques that are specific for the treatment of psychiatric disorders. *The Journal of Alternative & Complementary Medicine, 10*(1), 91–101.

Surawy, C., Roberts, J., & Silver, A. (2005). The effect of mindfulness training on mood and measures of fatigue, activity, and quality of life in patients with chronic fatigue syndrome on a hospital waiting list: A series of exploratory studies. *Behavioural and Cognitive Psychotherapy, 33*(1), 103–109.

Tedeschi, R. G. & Calhoun, L. G. (1995). *Trauma and transformation: Growing in the aftermath of suffering.* Thousand Oaks, CA: Sage Publications.

Vishnevsky, T., Cann, A., Calhoun, L. G., Tedeschi, R. G., & Demakis, G. J. (2010). Gender differences in self-reported posttraumatic growth: A meta-analysis. *Psychological of Women Quarterly, 34*(1), 110–120.

Wanden-Berghe, R. G., Sanz-Valero, J., & Wanden-Berghe, C. (2011). The application of mindfulness to eating disorders treatment: A systematic review. *Eating Disorders: The Journal of Treatment & Prevention, 19*(1), 34–48.

Wang, T., Hung, C. C. Y., & Randall, D. J. (2006). The comparative physiology of food deprivation: From feast to famine. *Annual Review of Physiology, 68*(1), 223–251.

Weick, K. E. (1995). *Sensemaking in organizations* (Vol. 3). Thousand Oaks, CA: Sage.

Werdel, M. B., Dy-Liacco, G. S., Ciarocchi, J. W., Wicks, R. J., & Breslford, G. M. (2014). The unique role of spirituality in the process of growth following stress and trauma. *Pastoral Psychology, 63*, 57–71.

Worthington, E. L. (2006). *Forgiveness and reconciliation: Theory and application.* New York: Routledge.

10 Clinical Application

While much of the methodology of clinical implementation for the model presented in this book is drawn from Pinsof's (1995, 2005) integrative problem-centered therapy, other aspects are developed in particular for work with anorexia nervosa in men and boys. After a brief overview of negative explanation, which is fundamental to the approach described here, we lay out four therapeutic orientations and three implementation contexts. In addition, we explain the rationale behind the model's treatment sequence, a prescribed way of moving through therapeutic orientations and contexts from superficial to deep levels of constraint in the problem-maintenance space. Finally, we bring these ideas to life through reference to a complex clinical case.

Negative Explanation

Drawing on theories of cybernetics, Bateson (1972) distinguished between positive and negative explanation. Positive explanations ask why human systems have problems, whereas negative explanations ask what keeps human systems from solving their problems (Breunlin, 1999). For example, a clinician relying on positive explanation would wonder what makes a boy with anorexia nervosa refuse food. In contrast, a clinician seeking a negative explanation would ask what keeps the boy from eating.

Although there are benefits and drawbacks to both positive and negative explanation, the integrative model presented in this book relies on negative explanation. In particular, for each patient system encountered in clinical practice, this model is used to generate a unique list of constraints (incorporated into the problem-maintenance space discussed in Chapter 2: An Integrative Approach) that prevent that patient system's identified patient from recovering from anorexia nervosa.

Clinical Implementation

In integrative problem-centered therapy, all psychotherapeutic approaches have a context and an orientation. Three *contexts*, or modalities, specify which members of the patient system are receiving direct services. The *individual* context targets a single person. In the *couple* context, at least two people from the same generation are receiving direct services. This includes homosexual, sibling, premarital, heterosexual, and friendship couples. In the *family–community* context, at least two people from different generations are receiving direct services. This includes nuclear and extended family as well as the immediate community, such as school, work, and friends.

The *orientation* of a psychotherapeutic approach specifies its theories of problem formation and problem resolution. The theory of problem formation explains how psychological and psychiatric problems are maintained. The theory of problem resolution delineates the processes and procedures for resolving psychological and psychiatric problems. In this model, we utilize four orientations.

First, the *engagement and alliance orientation* emphasizes the importance of general therapeutic skills in engaging the patient system in the treatment process and building a working alliance with the direct patient system. The importance of the stage of change of various members of the patient system is incorporated into this orientation. These issues are discussed in depth in Chapter 3: Diagnosis, Engagement, and Alliance.

Second, the *biobehavioral orientations* use either behavioral or biological interventions to change biological constraints on the biological level of the problem-maintenance space. Examples of this orientation include psychopharmacology, psychoeducation, and nutritional rehabilitation. Many of these orientations are discussed in Chapter 5: The Biological Metaframework.

Third, the *systemic orientation* addresses the systemic constraints within the patient system. This orientation recognizes that the underlying rules and structures in various systems – whether the family system, the parental subsystem, or in the treatment team itself – often constrain problem resolution. Examples of systemic orientations include structural family therapy (e.g., Minuchin, Rosman, & Baker, 1978), the Milan approach (Selvini Palazzoli, 1974), and the Maudsley approach to family-based treatment (e.g., Dare & Eisler, 1997). These orientations are discussed in Chapter 4: The Systemic Metaframework.

Finally, the *psychodynamic orientation* addresses a wide range of phenomena richly described by psychoanalytic theory, including drives and defense mechanisms, the role of transference and countertransference in treatment, the importance of internal object relations in coloring our experience of others, ways of regulating self-esteem, and the rich meanings that become attached to food, eating, and the body. This orientation is addressed specifically in Chapter 8: The Psychodynamic Metaframework.

As shown in Figure 10.1, the 3 contexts cut across the 4 orientations, creating 12 cells that represent specific domains of expertise (Pinsof, 1995).

Orientations	Contexts		
	Family–community	Couple	Individual
Engagement and alliance			
Biobehavioral			
Systemic			
Psychodynamic			

Figure 10.1 Problem-centered orientation–context matrix

Source: Adapted from Pinsof (1995)

Each orientation can be used in three different contexts – family–community, couple, and individual – which determines who is directly and consistently engaged in treatment.

Treatment Sequence

Following Pinsof (1995), the universal and preferred sequence of conceptualization and intervention progresses from the upper left to the lower right quadrant of the matrix. In this progression, the sequence moves from more superficial to deeper constraints, which allows for more efficient treatment. Because new constraints are discovered as treatment proceeds, however, it is often necessary to return to previous orientations and contexts at later stages of the treatment process.

When the patient system presents for treatment, the first task always involves solidifying treatment engagement and beginning to develop a working alliance with all members of the patient system – first with the family and community, which includes other treatment providers as well as important others such as coaches and teachers, then with the couple subsystem and, finally, with the identified patient himself.

With engagement in place and alliance building in process, the first question a clinician must ask is, "Is the patient in serious physical danger?" If so, medical interventions are often immediately required. For this reason, the biobehavioral orientations are next on the grid. Even if the patient is not in immediate medical risk, constraints at the biological level are inevitably present and need to be addressed through referral to appropriate providers, such as family doctors, psychiatrists, and nutritionists.

The systemic orientation comes next. In many cases, systemic factors may constrain the identified patient's ability to fully make use of individual treatment or prevent other members of the patient system from serving as a resource in the treatment process. In addition, in the early stages of treatment, family-based therapy is the gold standard for weight restoration (Lock & Le Grange, 2015). Finally, psychodynamic therapy is utilized to work with the intrapsychic factors that maintain disordered eating behavior, attitudes toward food, weight, and shape, and other problematic factors in the patient's psyche. This orientation often comprises the majority of the longer-term component of the treatment effort.

Clinical Case Study

Mrs. Dianne Lawrence contacts me by phone one afternoon to discuss her son, John, after locating my private practice through an Internet search engine. In a brief phone conversation, Dianne admits that she "doesn't know where to turn for help" about her intense worry and confusion for her son, who is "getting thinner and thinner." In our first conversation, I emphasize the importance of all family members attending the intake meeting, which we schedule for the following day. When the appointment time comes, however, only Dianne and John appear. Dianne informs me that her husband, Paul, is not available due to work obligations that cannot be rescheduled.

John is a 15-year-old African American male whose sense of personal style, reflected in his spikey hair and colorful attire, betrays his interest in fashion and design. According to his mother, John often spends hours on his art projects each day and hopes to pursue a long-term career in the industry. According to Dianne, her brother, Arthur, is a fashion designer who has served as an important mentor to John and has been enthusiastic about John's talent and potential. At present, as we will see, John is deeply entrenched in his struggle with anorexia nervosa. At our first meeting, John stands at 5' 11" and is 110 lbs. With a body mass index (BMI) of 15.3, John is significantly underweight.

John's mother is alarmed because, at a recent dental checkup, John's dentist was concerned that the enamel on his teeth had begun to decay. When questioned, John reported, with a flat affect, that he had been trying to lose weight for almost a year. Before then, John's weight had been 130 lbs at about 5' 9" tall. Although John believes he was "fat" at this weight, at a BMI of 20.4 I suspect he was at a healthy weight.

While concerned that Paul is not able to attend our initial interview, especially given his son's urgent need for treatment, after several inquiries during the initial meeting I gather that Dianne is reluctant to discuss the situation with her son present. As the initial interview draws to a close, I schedule a time to meet with Dianne the following day. In that meeting, she discloses that she and her husband are having marital problems that interfere with their ability to communicate about their son's struggles. With tears beginning to form, she confides that Paul has just informed her of his involvement in an extra-marital affair with a colleague named Stacy. In addition, Dianne informs me that Paul "doesn't believe in therapy" and feels her son should "toughen up."

Patient system	
Direct patient system	**Indirect patient system**
John (identified patient)	Paul
Dianne	Stacy
	Arthur (Dianne's brother)

Figure 10.2 Lawrence family patient system

As our conversation draws to a close, Dianne confides in me that she has struggled with her weight for a number of years. She worries about the impact of this on John and, in particular, reports that she has often worried aloud and joked about needing to go to a "fat farm" throughout John's childhood. I validate Dianne's desire to address her own struggles with food and weight and to explore their impact on her son, highlighting this as an important topic of conversation during future meetings.

At this early stage of treatment, the patient system takes the following shape, described in Figure 10.2. Notably, Stacy is a member of the indirect patient system because, in disrupting the communication and problem-solving capacities of the parental subsystem, she clearly constrains the resolution of John's anorexia nervosa. In addition, Dianne's brother, Arthur, is included in the indirect patient system because of the emotional importance that John appears to attach to him as a mentor and role model.

Engagement and Alliance Orientation

Beginning with the first phone call, I adopt the *engagement and alliance orientation*, which emphasizes engaging all members of the direct patient system in the treatment process and building working alliances. At this stage, I seek to engage and build an alliance with the Lawrence family itself, the parental/couple subsystem (Dianne and Paul) and, finally, with each member of the direct patient system – John, Dianne, at this point in treatment. After the initial interview, I am confident that both John and Dianne are engaged in treatment and that the alliance-building process is at work. Thus, an early task is to move Paul to the direct patient system and to begin forming a working alliance with him.

After meeting with Dianne, I call Paul to discuss his son's situation. While he is surprised to hear from me, when I express my concern about his son's well-being, he agrees to come in for a session. In our first conversation, Paul admits his concern about his son's welfare. Immediately, I begin to address the obstacles to John's engagement in the treatment process – in particular, his belief that men don't get eating disorders and that psychotherapy runs counter to his notions of "being a man." Means of addressing these issues are discussed at length in Chapter 3: Diagnosis, Engagement, and Alliance.

In addition, Paul and I discuss the importance of finding a way to help the parental subsystem work together. The following week, I meet with the couple together. Both members of the couple agree that their marital difficulties, including but not limited to Paul's extra-marital affair, have made it difficult for them to operate as a team in their son's care. With this in mind, I raise the possibility of working with a couples therapist. While Paul is ambivalent about "working on the marriage," I insist that regardless of whether the marriage continues, it is essential that Paul and Dianne find a way to operate as a team in the service of their son's treatment. The couple agrees, somewhat reluctantly, to meet with a couples therapist a few times.

During this period, I also begin meeting with John individually. Beginning with our first meeting, I am able to engage him in spirited conversation, especially about his passion for art and design. In spite of this, John is deeply ambivalent about the possibility of change. For John, being thin has become an "aesthetic choice" that is highly valued in the fashion industry and, he confides in me, an important aspect of his identity as a gay youth, an identity that he has only recently claimed for himself. At the same time, John can intellectually acknowledge that he is suffering from anorexia nervosa. Indeed, he admits that being fit, even thin, is significantly different than malnourished; however, his eating disorder has taken on a life of its own that will take considerable time to address.

Beginning with the initial interview, I am developing problem-maintenance space for the Lawrence family. Throughout the course of treatment, I will revise the problem-maintenance space as constraints are resolved and discovered. At the present stage of treatment, the problem-maintenance space is as shown in Figure 10.3.

Biobehavioral Orientation

The biobehavioral orientations are now applied. These orientations use either behavioral or biological interventions to change constraints on the biological level of the problem-maintenance space. At this point, two constraints have been identified at the biological level of the problem-maintenance space, as indicated in Figure 10.3. In particular, these constraints lie in the individual context.

Early on, I refer John to a dentist in an effort to repair existing damage and find ways to prevent further dental decay as his underlying malnutrition is addressed. Second, I refer John to a registered dietician and insist he have an immediate meeting with his family physician. These treatment providers will be able to provide specific guidance and expertise around the medical complexities involved in nutritional rehabilitation.

Systemic
Collaborative problem solving of parental subsystem is constrained by Paul's extra-marital affair.
John may be constrained from developing healthy attitudes about weight by his mother's ongoing struggle with being overweight.

Biological
John's capacity for problem-solving conversations (i.e., without obsessive and repetitive features) is constrained by his physical state of starvation.
John's dental health is constrained by his physical state of starvation.

Culture and gender
John's ability to develop healthy attitudes about weight and shape is constrained by problematic aspects of his cultural surround and personal interests (fashion and design).
Paul's beliefs about masculinity constrain help-seeking behavior for his son.

Psychodynamic
None identified.

Spiritual
None identified.

Figure 10.3 Lawrence family problem-maintenance space

Systemic Orientation

The systemic orientation is now applied. Early in treatment, Dianne and Paul were referred to a couples therapist in an effort to help them find ways to improve their teamwork (in particular, to increase Paul's involvement in the parental subsystem) and, over time, to resolve the problems in their marriage. Indeed, Paul's involvement in an extra-marital affair presented a considerable constraint to both Paul's involvement in the family and collaborative problem-solving in the parental subsystem.

As described in Chapter 4: The Systemic Metaframwork, we utilized family-based therapy to help Dianne and Paul take an active role in guiding John's nutritional rehabilitation. In collaboration with a nutritionist and family doctor, Dianne and Paul are increasingly able to provide the guidance and containment that their son needs during this anxiety-provoking process. After a year has passed, John's weight is 140 lbs at 5' 11". While his parents and dietician still closely monitor his eating, John is no longer at a medically dangerous low weight. And while John's self-esteem remains linked to being thin and many of the personality traits that contributed to his development of anorexia nervosa are still in place, he is beginning to recognize his body's need for nourishment and, furthermore, he is beginning to value responding appropriately to that need.

Early in treatment, I refer Dianne to an individual therapist, encouraging her to address the roots of her own lifelong struggle with food and weight. And in a later family session, Dianne acknowledges her struggle to both Paul and John, taking responsibility for any impact this may have had on the family. At this point, we also decide to move Dianne's brother, Arthur, into the direct patient system. Over the past year, John has "come out" to his parents and, in family sessions, admitted his insecurities about being a gay, African-American male. For several sessions, Arthur, who is also a gay man, is able to join John and me for several heartfelt conversations. Indeed, Arthur serves as an important role model in John's full recovery from anorexia nervosa over the coming years.

Psychodynamic Orientation

The psychodynamic orientation is employed to work with the intrapsychic factors that constrain the resolution of disordered eating behavior, attitudes toward food, weight, and shape, and other problematic factors in the patient's psyche. Throughout the treatment, I have been meeting weekly with John for individual psychotherapy. While much of our early work together was supportive in nature, attempting to help John to clarify his thoughts and feelings as he moves through stages of change in his recovery, toward the end of our treatment John began to raise questions unrelated to weight in our sessions.

In particular, John complained of his mother's continued "intrusive" behavior. For example, she insisted on "proof-reading and correcting" his college application essays. While he raised these concerns tentatively at first, through continued exploration of the dynamics of John's early relationships, their impact on his current experience of the world began to emerge. We discovered that underneath John's deference toward his mother was an intense fear of abandonment. This formed an important constraint on the psychodynamic level of the problem-maintenance space. Over the following year, John began, first in small and then in larger ways, to assert his independence from his mother, while also remaining connected to her. While this process was often anxiety provoking and difficult, the family, relying on their relationships with various treatment providers, was able to gather the support they needed to successfully move through the experience.

In addition, John and I began to explore the sources of his self-esteem, especially his intense dependence on validation from others in order to feel attractive and desirable. Over time, John and I were able to recognize his competence in many domains, artistic and otherwise. As John's self-esteem became increasingly grounded in a wide variety of relationships and personal attributes, many of his struggles with food, weight, and shape appeared to dissipate, especially his reliance on being thin as a source of self-esteem.

This stage of the treatment continued for several years. With his departure for college only weeks away, John and I met to review his gains in treatment, which we both agreed were considerable. Indeed, John had made enormous steps toward regaining his physical and psychological health. While his parents were now divorced, he maintained a close relationship with each of them. Indeed, although his parents' separation had precipitated considerable grief, it had also significantly decreased the overt conflict in his family and, now, his parents were able to operate as a team. And while John's self-esteem did not feel as solid as we would have liked, he now had a better understanding of the "triggers" that left him feeling vulnerable. We agreed that John should check in from time to time, both with his treatment team and with his parents, who had considerably more attunement to their son's emotional well-being than originally. We agreed that his future looked bright.

As this case illustrates, anorexia nervosa is a complex illness with both physical and psychological components that impact many layers of the patient system. In this book, we capture this complexity with an integrative model, which recognizes that the disorder has systemic, biological, cultural, psychodynamic, and spiritual components, each of which has been discussed in its own chapter. To address the complexity of a multi-layered patient system, four orientations are employed to resolve the factors that prevent the patient system from successfully moving toward full recovery.

Equally important, as has been highlighted through the book, anorexia nervosa manifests in men and boys differently than in women and girls. These differences show up in unique ways at each level of the problem-maintenance space and must be accounted for if the disorder is to be recognized and addressed. Furthermore, anorexia nervosa is intertwined with the entire patient system – the identified patient himself, certainly, but equally important, with his parents, family, and the larger community. By recognizing this fact, we conceptualize anorexia nervosa as a complex and multi-faceted problem that encompasses far more than low weight and problematic attitudes about food and eating. Ultimately, anorexia nervosa confronts all of us with a profound form of human suffering that must be fully understood and responded to in all of its complexity.

References

Bateson, G. (1972). *Steps to an ecology of mind: Collected essays in anthropology, psychiatry, evolution, and epistemology*. San Francisco, CA: Chandler Pub. Co.

Breunlin, D. C. (1999). Toward a theory of constraints. *Journal of Marriage and Family Therapy, 25*(3), 365–382.

Dare, C. & Eisler, I. (1997). Family therapy for anorexia nervosa. In D. M. Garner & P. E. Garfinkel (Eds.), *Handbook of treatment for eating disorders* (2nd ed.). New York: The Guilford Press.

Lock, J. & Le Grange, D. (2015). *Treatment manual for anorexia nervosa: A family-based approach*. New York: Guilford Publications.

Minuchin, S., Rosman, B. L., & Baker, L. (1978). *Psychosomatic families: Anorexia nervosa in context*. Boston, MA: Harvard University Press.

Pinsof, W. M. (1995). *Integrative problem-centered therapy: A synthesis of family, individual, and biological therapies*. New York: Basic Books.

Pinsof, W. M. (2005). Integrative problem-centered therapy. In J. C. Norcross & M. R. Goldfried (Eds.), *Handbook of psychotherapy integration* (pp. 282–402). New York: Oxford University Press.

Selvini Palazzoli, M. (1974). *Self-starvation*. London: Chaucer.

Index